THE
LIMITS
OF MY
LANGUAGE

THE
LIMITS
OF MY
LANGUAGE

EVA MEIJER

*Translated from the Dutch
by Antoinette Fawcett*

PUSHKIN PRESS

Pushkin Press
Somerset House, Strand
London WC2R 1LA

Original text © Eva Meijer 2019 and Uitgeverij Cossee BV, Amsterdam
English translation © Antoinette Fawcett 2021

The Limits of My Language was first published as *De grenzen van mijn taal* by
Uitgeverij Cossee in Amsterdam, 2019

First published by Pushkin Press in 2021

This publication has been made possible with financial support from the
Dutch Foundation for Literature.

**N ederlands
letterenfonds
dutch foundation
for literature**

9 8 7 6 5 4 3 2

ISBN 13: 978-1-78227-599-2

Designed and typeset by Tetragon, London
Printed and bound in the United Kingdom by Clays Ltd, Elcograf S.p.A.

www.pushkinpress.com

CONTENTS

INTRODUCTION

An ending. An encasing, a world within a world (a self inside a self), thoughts that thrust themselves into a nest of other thoughts and ruthlessly push out their healthy foster-brothers and sisters (like baby cuckoos), an ever-present shadow (even in the light), a confirmation, a truth, an illusion, heavy sand where the shore turns to sea, a fungus that manages to worm its spores into everything, static noise, fading away, a greyness that sucks up every colour, until all that's left is the memory of colour.

Depression is like mourning, and mourning can cause depression. It's like grief and fear, too, generic terms for what happens when you lose something, or are afraid of losing something; for when you fall, or have already fallen. But depression is also different: it's coupled to another kind of loss—the loss of reality. Life-changing events make you see the world differently—when you fall in love, you gain a whole new world; when you lose someone, you lose a world too—and such events can make you feel that you're a completely different person. Yet you're still involved in the world; you're rooted in it, even if you can't recognize it for the time being. You're still yourself. But depression makes you doubt the connection between yourself and the world: it's not only that you no longer feel at home in it, but also that you realize there's no such thing as a safe place, a home. Depression can affect your brain and the meaning of your life, like a rot eating into your days. After the first episode of depression you have a more-than-average chance of a second episode, and after two periods of depression it's more likely than not that you'll get depressed again, and in this way it can become a part of your life.

Around the end of 2017, during an argument, my partner chided me for being sad so often. This surprised me, because I didn't feel particularly sad at that point: the melancholy that goes along with my life was there, but not more than usual. And I certainly wasn't depressed. I'm absolutely sure about that because for part of my life I have been depressed. Not long after the argument I read a book in which the writer, someone who has a physical disability, said very clearly that she wouldn't want to live without it, and I wondered what my own take on this was. For a long time I thought my life wasn't worth living because the unhappiness often weighed so much more than the happiness. I don't mean that there's never been any beauty in my life—the opposite, in fact—but for a good part of it my spirits have been well below par. That is something I wouldn't wish on anyone. At the same time, the experience has enriched my view of the world and I've developed a good work ethic. I live inside my work. I don't know if depression has given me more empathy and imagination, and made me more sensitive: it could also be that these qualities preceded the depression, and that they are a part of the cause. At any rate, these events set me thinking.

This essay is the result: a brief philosophical investigation into depression, in which I use my own experiences as material. This is not so I can lay myself completely bare, without holding back a single detail, as Rousseau says he will do at the beginning of his *Confessions*. I don't want to make a completely faithful picture of my own life up to this point, or to create a self-portrait; I'm using my life as a lens to investigate the structure and significance of depression. This is just a fraction of all I could say about myself (and deeds that are put into words always diverge from the underlying events). Nevertheless, depression is an important aspect of my life, and something that has strongly shaped me.

I don't think that a better understanding of what depression is can cure people. But it does have value.

Depression is more than a chemical problem—the questions that occupy someone with depression are fundamentally human, and they touch on other philosophical questions that concern language, autonomy, power relations, loneliness, and the relationship between body and mind. But this essay is also about the other side, such as animals, trees, others, art: about consolation, and hope, and the things that can give life meaning.

1

On the seeping away of colour and death at the dinner table: a brief history

May 1994 was unusually warm and sunny, as I remember it.[1] My classmates sat around on the grass every break time, making daisy chains and playing the guitar—the world glowed and life was full of promise. But as they skipped merrily through life, each step I took made me sink further and further into deep, invisible mud. It was as if the force of gravity was too strong, as if the earth was dragging me under. I was fourteen and that feeling of bleakness was something I'd long known.

On my eighth birthday, for example, one of my aunts took me to a toyshop where I could choose a present for myself. I picked a plush dog in a basket, which had little puppies with it. I thought it was really sweet, but at the same time I had the feeling that I hadn't chosen well,

EVA MEIJER

that I should have picked something more sensible. My birthday wasn't pleasant; there was an argument, and a strange grey atmosphere crept into the day. I sensed something wasn't right—so how could other people pretend it was? That feeling kept coming and going throughout my childhood, until that month of May when it came into the foreground and pushed other things further and further back.

May turned to June and everything grew greyer, like in a cartoon film in which colour gradually seeps from the surroundings until everything is black and white. Then, in the black and white that followed, the contrast faded: the white became less clear and finally the grey just bled into grey. The world around me became a different world, in which things wouldn't simply turn out well, in which it was actually more likely that they'd never turn out well again. While my body was being taken over by that weight, my thoughts clumped around a single theme: it would be better if I didn't exist. For many years afterwards I detested May, the smell of spring, the green and the growth, and I still don't feel happy at the first signs of summer—unlike some people, I can't look forward to what is on the way.

Around that time I first read Jean-Paul Sartre's *Nausea*,[2] in which the main character, Roquentin, has exactly the same feeling of pointlessness. I found it a very frightening book. It was as if what I was feeling, and what Sartre

12

described, touched on a barren truth, a desolation, which now that I'd discovered it would never go away. For Sartre, that barrenness isn't purely bad: it's also the starting point of freedom. According to him human beings aren't simply bodies, we are also consciousnesses, and to rise above our physical situatedness we must confront the absurdity and emptiness of existence. This shouldn't be camouflaged with the idea of a god, the illusion of consolation, or by wanting to fulfil other people's wishes: you have to will yourself free. It is by making your own choices and taking responsibility for them that you can achieve self-realization. But I didn't know about that freedom then. I read about Roquentin doing his historical research in the library, about his increasing sense of alienation and his consequent realization that this has nothing to do with him, but is simply what the world is like. His nausea is not a reaction to random events, but is a symptom of his growing understanding of existence. Those who believe in goodness and beauty, like the Autodidact, who is often in the library as well, are simply naïve and gullible. And we'll find nothing behind the bad things; don't fool yourself.

Teenagers and existentialists understand something true, something bleak about life. Perhaps children don't live in a safe world—it is already the real world, a world where cats are killed by cars, animals are eaten, and other children experience war (or they themselves, in many parts of the world)—but often they haven't yet acquired the hardness of adults, or the habituation of the adult to that hardness. Their world is magical and alive, everything is still possible. For the adolescent, however, the world presents itself with full force. Falling in love for the first time can create a sense of limitlessness; feeling is something that flows out from you, in every direction. Life's lack of meaning can present itself in this way too: this is how it is, this is the truth about life, and everyone who simply enjoys it is labouring under an illusion.

I thought things would never get better, that I'd always feel that way, and in addition to the various feelings of guilt I had, I was constantly thinking about death. Death, my own death, acquired a shape in those days, like a shadow that was always at my side. My plans weren't concrete, but at the same time they were constantly present. I talked about it, with my friends and at school, and with various therapists who thought that things would sort themselves out. In those days I liked wearing bright clothes and that was one of the reasons why I wasn't taken seriously by all the different psychologists and psychiatrists I consulted. One of them literally wrote that it couldn't be all that bad, because I was wearing a green woolly hat with a butterfly on it, instead of just wearing black, and anyway, according to him, I was gifted in all sorts of ways. I drank a lot, skipped school and argued with my teachers, and

I sang. That all helped a little, and just managed to carry me through the days. I didn't have the feeling I was ill: I thought I was bad, and the things I did were aimed at getting rid of that feeling, or setting it aside. Night after night, I sat by the window smoking roll-ups and listening to music, while I wrote poems and songs, and letters, which I sometimes burnt. Everything whirled around a chasm: this is how it is, I am alone here, everything I do is wrong—and then again.

Philosophical and concrete suicide

In *The Myth of Sisyphus* Albert Camus wonders whether understanding that life is meaningless should necessarily lead to suicide.[3,4] According to him this question, whether or not we should commit suicide, is the fundamental philosophical problem. Life is chaotic and arbitrary and absurd: we ask, and the world is unreasonably silent; it does not give us the meaning or purpose we long for. You could respond to this by believing in a god who has shaped the universe in his or her own image and invested it with order and purpose. Or you can accept that life is meaningless and make the leap into death, because its lack of meaning makes life not worth living. There is, however, a third option: to embrace absurdity. In a world in which absurdity prevails we, as humans, can choose to confront the absurd, as well as the contradiction it brings: wanting to fight against it, wanting to break free from it, although this is also absurd. If we do this, then suicide isn't the solution, but rather choosing to live as broadly and richly as possible: like Don Juan, who pursues his passions pointlessly, but with whole-hearted conviction; like the actor who lives through countless human lives; like the artist who doesn't attempt to give meaning to absurdity, but represents it exactly as it is.

Camus is right, of course, when he argues that we should embrace absurdity. That life is absurd is also a source of joy, and humour is one of our best weapons against its lack of meaning. But this is also one of the areas where things can go wrong when you're depressed: you can no longer appreciate the value of that absurdity, or its fun. Relationships lose their meaning, and so does art; you become cut off from yourself and from the world. I had good friends during my first depression, who knew what was happening to me, but that didn't help at all, because I thought I'd finally understood that I was alone and that was why I really was alone. My thoughts isolated me. And everything was grey; I was completely grey, just a husk for the feeling I had. No one else could see that everything was grey now, or how I really was—anything sweet that others did for me only confirmed my own self-hatred. And there wasn't any prospect of things changing. Sometimes my mother would say that your school days are the best days of your life.

In spite of skipping school and behaving badly, I passed my final exams without any problems, and then I went to England to study singing. A new start, rooted in the past. A few months later my aunt took her own life. It wasn't entirely unexpected; she'd had serious neuralgia for a long time and we knew she didn't want to carry on like that; she had made a half-hearted suicide attempt before. At the same time, it was totally unexpected, a lightning bolt that split the world in two: a before and an after. Death always splits the world in two, of course, but for me something really did shift in how I thought things fitted together. Things don't always get better; certain fractures still remain, more than twenty years later. The inconceivable can actually happen. I'm not talking about grief or sorrow. That was there too, of course, although my grief was as nothing compared to that of her mother, her sisters and her two daughters. But something really did break. I don't know whether suicide is worse than any other kind of death; that must depend entirely on who dies and how. It is different though, certainly in the case of someone whose treatment options haven't yet been exhausted, or barely explored, in fact. Then there are plenty of loud, harsh 'if I'd onlys' or 'if I'd just beens…'. In my aunt's case there are so many different ways that the tide could have been turned, or so it seems: not having left her alone on the day it happened; getting a psychiatrist to investigate her in the days and weeks before; getting her admitted into a specialist facility; or maybe medication could have helped. I never actually talked to her about her death wish.

The complete grief and misery after her death wasn't good for my state of mind, but it didn't change my ideas about suicide: suicide is an ending, not a solution. A solution presupposes that something good will come of it, that something of the old will shift into the new, while suicide only leads to the absence of the previous problem. I just think you shouldn't do this if you have children. At least, that wouldn't be my intention—I can't judge the depth of someone else's (unforeseen) suffering.

What I did see very clearly at that time was that suicide as a concrete act is far removed from the abstract philosophical question as to whether or not we should take our own lives. It's a desperate act, motivated by acute or sublimated despair, an act that often goes wrong,[5] with blood, injuries (sometimes permanent), and frightened family members and friends. If the attempt does succeed, then the survivors don't just have to sort out a coffin, funeral music, eulogies, money matters and other things, but they're also left with an enormous amount of guilt and distress. That guilt and distress leave traces, scored into the lives of all that are left behind. The edges eventually wear away, but they never vanish, just as grief never vanishes either, but simply changes form, and these traces carry on shaping everything that happens afterwards.

Carving out a place in the world

I don't actually think that whether or not we should take our own lives is the fundamental philosophical question— there are so many of them. But it is a question I carried with me for a long time. The depression that started when I was fourteen lasted about seven years, on and off. There are some years I can scarcely remember, from around the age of seventeen to twenty. Lost time, probably still stored somewhere inside me. Since I turned twenty-one, there have been other periods when things went badly for me, but never again for such a long stretch—sometimes for just a few months, a couple of times for about a year and a half. I bear in mind that I may become depressed again, but it's been going pretty well for quite some time. For me, 'pretty well' never means that it's completely light—I carry the darkness with me, to a greater or lesser extent. That's not to say that nothing good or nice ever happens to me—my life is a rich one. And I always have the feeling that things are going very well as long as I'm not actually depressed, even if that's not necessarily the case.

In the first weeks of the ethics module in philosophy at the University of Amsterdam, the focus is on hedonism and utilitarianism, schools of thought that take happiness as the main measure of value. That was something that made me stumble as a student, and it did so again when I was teaching there. Putting aside the question as to whether this is indeed a sensible way of thinking about ethics, it surprised me that people can really be happy, or that they aspire to it. As far as I'm concerned, it's not a good idea to build a life on the pursuit of happiness, although I do like contributing to the happiness of others.

One element of learning how to deal with depression is looking elsewhere for what is valuable. What eventually saved me was my work.[6,7] I learnt how to link my destiny to what I was making and because of that I could put in brackets the question of whether I should die, and to a certain extent I could also do that with how I was feeling. This doesn't have much to do with being cured; it means adopting an attitude to something that is given to you. My work gives my life meaning, and working gives me and my days their shape. I've taught myself a routine that keeps me going. It makes a difference that I'm an optimistic depressive: I have the urge to realize myself and I'm disciplined and militant. And the beauty of the work I do is that my feelings can flow into what I create. I wrote the final section of my novel *The Peacock Butterfly*,[8] for example, at a time when I could do little else except describe what was dragging me down. Many of my songs are about falling, and the darkness sometimes sneaks into my drawings. I usually work too hard, or harder than most people, at any rate, but that's good—it's better to be tired than dead. I've trained myself to live like this and it works. For someone for whom being.alive isn't all that self-evident, it's already quite something to be able to cultivate this sort of attitude.

The first things I wrote were songs. In her song 'The Letter', Kristin Hersh describes what it's like to be imprisoned in your own head: 'September 29th, 1984, Dear so and so, gather me up because I'm lost, or I'm back where I started from, I'm crawling on the floor, rolling on the ground.' Accompanied by the same two chords throughout, Hersh sings a room to life, a hotel room maybe, a place where the person she is singing to isn't present and can't be present: the room is in her head. She can't get out of it. It's not just a song, it's a ritual, an incantation; by singing she creates a space where there is no space.[9] When I was a teenager, I listened a lot to Hersh's *Hips and Makers*, the album which includes this song, sitting on the windowsill, smoking. I listened a lot to other singer-songwriters too, and I started to write songs myself and perform them. Singing helps you to open your heart: the risk with illnesses of the head is that your heart shuts completely. My songs created a bridge between the outside world and me, and through singing them I kept on conquering the distance.[10] When I sang, I existed.

Self-portraits and being present/absent

The American photographer Francesca Woodman, who at the age of twenty-two committed suicide by jumping off a roof, made countless self-portraits in which she is simultaneously present and absent.[11] In these black-and-white photos her body, often naked, is both the material and the subject. Mostly she's moving, just gone or almost gone when the photo is taken: there are imprints left in the earth, or on the floor of a house; you can still see her in a mirror, or see just a part of her arms or legs. They're a kind of apparition, showing something about the way we as mortal beings are preserved, and how we get lost. (Photography is, of course, the quintessential art of preservation: we snip a moment out of time so that everyone can keep seeing it for ever, which only emphasizes that it has already passed.) The photos reproduce the twilight zone between being here and having been here. They are traces. In this respect, they are reminiscent of the body-prints of the Cuban-American artist Ana Mendieta.[12] Her *Silueta* series consists of body-prints in the earth, vanished female bodies in sand, sometimes partially coloured with red pigment. We've always been here, Mendieta says, and we'll always depart. Woodman and Mendieta's work shows what comes after the material form and what remains of it. Even when their own bodies come into view, they're a part of something greater into which they're already fading.[13]

For a long time I didn't want to forget anything. That's why I started making my work—songs are solidified feeling; words on paper become something not stronger than I am, perhaps, but more lasting, and they'll lead a life of their own, separate from me.[14] Wanting not to forget things was related to my love of death, my own death, which often perched on a little stool somewhere in the corner of my room, and to the fact that this love terrified me. But it was mainly linked to knowing that everything vanishes. As I grow older, the desire to preserve things is diminishing and I'm more able to surrender to everything that keeps moving. Perhaps that's also a loss. The cyclical carries its own sadness, you have to be able to bear that.[15]

At art school, and in the years before and after, I mainly made self-portraits, not out of vanity, but to give myself form, and to investigate what that actually is—a self. I was also investigating my own body, the form that I had.[16] Jeanette Winterson, writing about *Strangeland*,[17] Tracey Emin's hyper-intimate and lyrical memoir, says there's never any borderline between life and work, not because all art is autobiographical, but because you always have to put all of yourself into what you create.[18] Self-portraits aren't any more personal or intimate than other work, they simply offer a special lens. For Emin, the line between life and work has always been fluid. Her life is, sometimes very literally, the subject of her art: growing up in Margate, her love life, her sex life, the difficult relationship with her family, her situation as an artist, a woman, an artist who is a woman.

One of her best-known installations is *My Bed*: a slept-in bed with white sheets, towels and a pair of tights, and a blue mat in front of it with all kinds of personal items: slippers, packets of cigarettes, a toy dog, a belt, vodka bottles, condoms, a tampon. This is her own bed, where she spent four days after a break-up. Without any food, but with plenty of alcohol and sex. *The Guardian* describes this work of art as a 'violent mix of sex and death',[19] and it does have a macho character (as Emin's work often does), while at the same time it's a bed, with soft sheets, which stands for nice things like dreaming and sleeping and making love, and your animal companion on your pillow. This is how bad it was, the bed says. It witnessed Emin's feelings, and the public is also a witness via the bed.

A bed is a good metaphor for depression, because depressions are often endured in bed, and because it's a place outside of real life. (I know many writers who work in bed, though, so it can also be a place of work.) It's the place of sleep, of dreaming, of between-time. When you're depressed all time is between-time or anti-time, just as the depressed person is a between-person, not dead but certainly not alive (if only you were actually dead or alive). Making an imprint of that, something real, putting the bed that rescued you inside a white space, might be the only sensible thing you can still do with it.

Nowadays I rarely make self-portraits any more, although I do speak through my work. Perhaps this is a kind of self-portrait. There are many misunderstandings about the difference between fiction and non-fiction, such as that one represents the truth and the other is purely fabrication. That isn't the case—fiction can be just as truthful as non-fiction, and sometimes even more so. Both approaches offer a different perspective on how to bring the chosen material into the spotlight and they can therefore complement each other. A story can represent a certain experience or condition quite differently than academic discourse or a biographical sketch and so it can involve the reader in a different way. It can be just as specific and precise in doing so. Certain things can be said better in one kind of language than another. Making something always has an element of translation in it and, as Winterson says, you should always do it with everything you have.

The aesthetics of suicide

Depression is relatively common among artists, and writers have up to fifty per cent more chance of committing suicide than ordinary people, as a large-scale Swedish study has revealed.[20] In her essay 'The life artist: towards an aesthetics of suicide' the Flemish writer and philosopher Patricia De Martelaere examines whether we can approach suicide as an aesthetic question.[21] She thinks that what lies behind the death wish of struggling yet successful writers is a longing for completion. Her reasoning is as follows. According to Freud, one of our greatest unconscious desires is to be present at our own funeral, which is why people often dream about it. De Martelaere believes that this points to the wish to bring life to a rounded conclusion, instead of being caught out by death. She names three writers, Hemingway, Plath and Pavese, all of whom were successful when they died, but who couldn't 'prevent themselves' from committing suicide. This suicidal type works hard, but then collapses, 'haunted by the need for experience, consciousness and control'.[22] In the end, they'd rather be dead, because life will then be perfect, in the sense of being fully perfected. The passion at the heart of this is aesthetic in nature. Suicide completes life and changes it into an experience, no longer for oneself, admittedly, but observable to others. Someone effectively signs off their life, and that is a starting shot for others to search for its full meaning. This rounding-off points to an artistic ideal, comparable to completing a novel, which also reveals a self-made world, a finished story.

In his memoir *Darkness Visible*, William Styron describes the experience of going to Paris, a city he adores, to receive the prestigious Prix Mondial Cino Del Duca for his complete oeuvre.[23] He consults a reputable psychiatrist before he goes, because he is already feeling deep hopelessness. The psychiatrist advises him to go, but to return home again as quickly as possible. Styron's state of mind deteriorates during the journey: unlike many depressed people he can still get out of bed in the morning, but he collapses in the course of the day (literally: he can barely stay upright). This gets worse when he's at home again. Medication makes his condition even graver, and his state deteriorates until his admission into hospital brings a turning point for him and he begins to recover.

Styron was contemplating suicide and came very close to it—he had already burnt his diaries—yet his account shows something very different to the freedom and especially the choice about dying that De Martelaere posits. He realizes that he has won an important prize, and that he's lucky to have a wife who always supports him, but he can no longer pull himself out of the mud that is dragging him down. Not all writers who commit suicide may have been depressed, but you'd expect that to be the case for quite a number of them. And when you're depressed killing yourself is not an aesthetic act; there's no room for aesthetics in such a situation, and to suggest that there is seems somewhat cruel.

Art can help give a shape to certain experiences and to life itself. It is something external (and this is true also for the artist) which provides meaning and can sometimes carry you. If your days have no worth at all, they can still give you the time to make something beautiful. Nevertheless, art isn't a solution, at the most it's an opening to something lighter—but in order to get there, you have to be able to move and set things in motion, something that people with depression often can't do.

The limits of freedom

The existentialists have a point, of course, when they argue that, from the perspective of eternity, life is meaningless—there is no god or goddess for whom we should do our best, we only have each other, and everyone will die.[24] That sharp, barren realization, which hit me so hard when I was a teenager—whatever thoughts it was wrapped in—is for me sometimes still the basis of depressive thinking.[25] But an existential approach to depression, or suicide, has its limits. The duty to be free, to will yourself to be free, can't be achieved at all if you're suffering from a severe depression. Realizing yourself, being the best person you can, entering into the world: none of these things are possible then. So although the existential tradition does offer certain insights, its creed can't be followed. Those thinking about committing suicide because life is unliveable can't, like Camus, choose to embrace the absurd—that can only happen later, if there is a later (when, like Emin, you get up, after four days in bed, or when you can read and write again, after being admitted to a clinic). This objection to existentialism doesn't only apply to thinking about depression: critics also argue that existentialists overestimate our capacity for freedom, because we are always, in various ways, bound to our own facticity, to what defines us both socially and physically. We are born into structures that help determine how our lives will progress—and our gender, skin colour, psychological and physical condition, social class, and all kinds of other factors play their part in this. We are bodies, and that is something we all have in common, with the other animals too, for that matter. This makes us vulnerable. This vulnerability isn't something to shake off or get rid of: it shows us that things are worth doing, and can be the start of encountering the other, who is completely different to us, yet is also mortal and rooted in this world.

2

On crooked trees and the shaping of the soul

Depressions affect the brain. The prefrontal cortex, located at the front of the skull, displays less activity during a depression. This is the part of the brain that controls cognitive and emotional functions. When it's not working properly, a loss of interest, poor concentration, impaired thinking, and feelings of distress and despair may arise. The hippocampus, which is responsible for our memories, loses volume—and that in turn leads to forgetfulness. In the centre of the brain the functioning of the thalamus is also disrupted. This is where sensory stimuli are processed, and this disruption can cause anxiety and agitation. Around the thalamus, the basal ganglia, like the hippocampus, start shrinking—this can slow down movement, because this is where motor activity is regulated. Older people who've had multiple episodes of depression have a more shrivelled hippocampus than others of their age.[26] Chronic depression is, therefore, harmful to the brain and probably makes it more susceptible to age-related diseases, such as dementia. Moreover, you're more likely to get such an illness if you first become depressed at an early age.[27] The rest of the body also ages faster for people with depressive disorders.[28]

So the brain of the depressed person changes, but how does the soul change? By 'soul' I don't mean an immortal, invisible spirit, but something similar to Wittgenstein's idea of it in his later work: someone; the one you talk to when you're talking to someone; a self that can't be reduced to consciousness or reason, and not purely to the body's reflexes either. For a long time philosophy focused primarily on people's heads, on their capacity for reason. But mind and body cannot be so easily separated. Our brains are matter and what we think is bound up with how we exist as bodies, all the way down. Our embodied selves, and how we understand them, are in turn shaped by the cultures in which we live and the material from which they're composed.

The blackest black, the whitest white

There was, in fact, quite a bit of depression in Wittgenstein's family.[29] Three of his four brothers are thought to have committed suicide, although the exact circumstances of the third brother's death are still unclear. (The fourth brother, Paul, was a concert pianist and lost a hand in the First World War, after which he continued performing, determined to shine even with one hand. Ravel wrote a piece for him, as did a number of other important composers of that period—but this is by the bye.) Wittgenstein himself also went through difficult patches—his letters sometimes give evidence of deep despair—and in the First World War he insisted on being sent to the front, and not because of his patriotism. Philosophy did not make him happy: he was never satisfied with his ideas and he set the bar so high that it was impossible to achieve what he had in mind. But philosophy was perhaps the opponent he needed to prevent things getting worse. His fanaticism comes across most clearly in the *Tractatus*, an edifice that tries to replicate the universe, in which, of course, it fails. (This book has one of the most moving conclusions of any work of philosophy, but to understand why that is, you have to read it in its totality.)[30] His later work displays more compassion for human failings.[31] He suddenly realizes that language, his way into the interpretation of reality, is not

33

a cast-iron system and that it carries our own contingency within it: language, like us, is unfinished, sometimes paradoxical, flawed, and at times opaque and illogical. But it works—and according to Wittgenstein we should focus on how it works if we want to understand anything at all about it. If we wish to investigate the meaning of a concept, then we should look at how people use it.

When people speak or write about depression they often use fine words to describe it. I've always had an aversion to comparing depression to monsters, demons or animals (and certainly to dogs, because how can they be blamed?), and I also dislike metaphors that use the colour black. Partly because images like these are clichés, partly because I see depression more as an absence than a presence. Everything worthwhile is slowly scraped away and all that remains is bare rock. Anxiety or grief often create a surplus of emotion, but depression, by contrast, weeds out the good feelings, making everything barer and emptier, and giving negative feelings free rein. While anxiety or grief are often to do with things that are worth bothering about, depression shows you that nothing is worthwhile. And a depression isn't black, let alone pitch-black. Dark, perhaps, just as night is dark when light has left the world, making your surroundings seem more dangerous, making you less able to orientate yourself—it's much quieter than during the day and what is still there is less noticeable.[32] If depression has a colour at all, it's more grey than anything else, and sometimes it's white. White is the colour of silence, of freezing cold, of being shut out, of nothing, of loss. If you mix all the colours together, then what apparently emerges is absence. White is also the colour of snow, of my cat Putih, and of endlessness, some of the most beautiful things I know, but in and of itself it is not a place you can inhabit. Nothing grows in white.[33]

The metaphor of fighting an illness, often also used with depression, has rightly received a great deal of criticism already. That is because it seems to put the responsibility on the person who is ill: if you don't get better, then you haven't fought hard enough, apparently. Yet getting better often has little to do with you, whether you have cancer or depression. It can feel like a battle, but the outcome isn't always affected by how hard you fight. You can be in continuous therapy, take your medicines, do all the right things, and yet remain deeply unhappy. It's a matter of chance if you get depressed, and it is often also a matter of chance how your depression develops, if you'll emerge from it, and whether you'll get depressed again. There are things you can do to cope with depression, as I'll discuss in the following chapters, but ultimately it's not just up to you.[34]

Metaphors aren't useless, of course. Imagine carrying a sea inside your body. It moves at every step, just enough to let you feel that you're made of water. You know the water is dangerous, that people have drowned in it, that you can't live beneath it. You also know you're stuck with that sea, and there's no escaping it. Sometimes the water rises, and then it falls again, like the tides, although not as regularly. Till one day it rises and rises and you slowly start to panic. You can't escape it, because it's inside you. No one sees it from your exterior, although your eyes fill with tears more than usual. You'd better lie down somewhere and wait till the water drops and you can move again. You'd better not lie down, because if you do you'll probably drown—and meanwhile the water is rising and you've already been holding your breath for a minute.

No, imagine that you once encountered your own death. Because you wanted to die, because you enticed it. No one can meet her own death without being physically touched by it, and since that time you've carried a shadow inside your body. If they cut you in two, it would be visible: a thin, black layer. On the outside, no one can see anything at all—at the most your skin is a little paler—but you can sense it, especially when you're tired or sad, and you know this will never change again.

Or imagine you're walking in a wood. It's a lovely day. This isn't the first time you've been here, but you haven't been very often either, and you choose a new route. There's nothing wrong with that, you know roughly how the paths branch. You turn left, and left again, and then right, and now you want to go back home. When you turn around you can't remember which path you came from. There are no clues—you think you recognize a tree, and feel a moment's relief, but then it turns out to be a different one. You start walking faster. In an hour it will be dusk. There's no signal on your phone. This will make a good story, you think, trying to calm yourself down—soon you'll be nice and cosy, back at home again. It isn't cold, you won't freeze to death if you don't get home on time. They'll realize you're missing and will come looking for you. But panic sneaks into your stomach, into your legs. The space around you changes and gets bigger. You grow smaller. There could be strangers hiding behind the trees. Your ears prick up, your eyes open wider, your breath quickens, and your heartbeat too. The scent of the wood is stifling, no longer soothing. It's already growing dark. You'll never get home again. You'll always stay stuck in this moment.

Growing crooked

Trees that develop without setbacks stand straight and proud. At first their branches grow upwards, then sideways, and finally a little downwards, so they can bend with the rain and snow. Most adult trees, however, have gone through something in their lives: another tree falling against them; branches broken by the weight of snow or ice; fungus; holes in their trunks made by woodpeckers or beetles. All these have changed their form and they've acquired scars. Our own lives are similar and our form results from all the things we have experienced. No one stays completely intact. A shrunken hippocampus limits us, but exactly how it does depends on the greater whole. Years filled with depressions are like scorched diaries in which only fragments can still be read, and the fear of a new episode of depression can linger on. But that isn't the only thing that defines someone.

In *Beasts of Burden*, a book about the relationship between the way we treat and perceive disabled people and nonhuman animals, Sunaura Taylor states that she wouldn't want to live without her disability.[35] Taylor was born with arthrogryposis multiplex congenita (AMC), a condition that means that the joints of the body are not attached to each other in the normal way. Her disability gives her a unique perspective on life, she says, and difference is richness. If we were all the same, the world would seem duller and more boring. She also says this isn't necessarily true for everyone: there are plenty of people who suffer terribly from their physical and mental disabilities and who would rather not have been born. This is also the case for a number of depressive people. It is difficult to see the point of a life with repeated, long-lasting depressions—with more periods of depression than good times. The complexity of illnesses that lodge in the mind is that they rob you of your normal way of thinking and your resistance, just as physical illnesses do to the body, so you can no longer see what the world is like. Not everyone becomes stronger from enduring something like this and not everyone can endure it.

It's true, though, that adverse and painful experiences are formative, as Taylor says, and that they give you a special outlook on life. I wouldn't wish my life on anyone else (certainly not specific periods of it), and yet I wouldn't want to swap it for any other life. This is mainly because what I do is so deeply connected to what I've experienced. I know what it's like to deviate from the norm (not only in the realm of madness) and I know what it is to suffer, which can help in understanding or accepting the suffering of others. What's more, depressions place you outside the world and give you the opportunity to view it from a distance. That is good for both the writer and the philosopher; it helps you make your own judgements. There's a lot wrong with the status quo and being able to think for yourself is very important. Because I had to work hard at being alive, I'm pretty immune to the opinions of others. Praise of my work doesn't make me proud and compliments mean very little to me (nor the reverse, in fact: a bad review doesn't affect me, because I'm always much more critical about my work than the most critical reader). In any case, it puts things into perspective. If death is sitting on the sofa beside you, all the other little problems matter less.

I don't exactly know how my depressions have changed me because I don't really know who I was before (there wasn't much of a 'before'), and I certainly don't know who I would otherwise have been. Michel Foucault, the French post-structuralist philosopher, has described care of the self as an ethical project.[36] We can cultivate ourselves by acquiring specific practices and techniques, thereby attaining a certain degree of freedom. This is similar to what Aristotle says in *The Nicomachean Ethics* about the development of virtue and the formation of character as a kind of training. According to Aristotle, acting virtuously isn't about moral precepts, or working out the right action on the basis of how much happiness we expect it to deliver. We should do good, and by often doing good you become a good person. Similarly, by living with depression, which can sometimes last a long time, you can try to become someone who can live with being depressed. That requires practice, a stoic attitude to what happens to you, and the ability to keep going. But I'll return to that later.

Gaps in the world

Many writers have written first-person accounts of their depression: William Styron, for example, whom I've already discussed; Elizabeth Wurtzel in *Prozac Nation*; or Andrew Solomon in his major work *The Noonday Demon*. Books like these are a kind of war reporting. They have something glorious about them: 'we've survived'; but also something ominous: 'watch out, there's always another war looming'. Like real war reports, they don't leave out the gory details, and they faithfully depict the sheer boredom of repeated episodes of depression, and how their wretchedness makes time drag on and on.

The philosopher Kevin Aho argues that such reports are essential for understanding exactly what depression is.[37] It's not enough to measure what kinds of biochemicals people produce or don't produce, or to look at their behaviour: to understand the experience of depression, and therefore also to be able to treat it, we have to listen to people who live with depression Their accounts reveal a different aspect of the illness. Aho's method of investigating depression, by looking at the personal experiences of people who actually have it, is based on the insights of phenomenology. Phenomenology investigates the structures of experience and consciousness, and bases itself on direct individual experience. Phenomenologists want to set our assumptions about the world inside brackets and to explore the way things appear to us, and how we are connected to them, through experience itself. To investigate depression in this manner means starting with the actual experience, and on that basis searching for its underlying structures.

According to Aho, depression interferes with normal experience in a number of different ways. Depressed people often experience a feeling of paralysis. They lose any sense of purpose in their lives, and get bogged down in a swampy present, detached from the rest of the world— they become uprooted. Being depressed cuts you off from your everyday environment and from the way you function within it. This makes it difficult to keep going and makes your life-world, your automatic sense of being at home in your environment, collapse.

The sensation of being suddenly hoisted out of your own habits, and experiencing them as strange, is something Martin Heidegger sees as being essential for humans.[38] He makes a distinction between the normal experience of fear or boredom and a deeper experience of these feelings, one which calls our whole existence into question. Being afraid of something, or getting bored while you're waiting for the train, is normal; things of this kind regularly happen to everyone. But sometimes such an experience suddenly makes you question yourself and your own existence. As an example, Heidegger describes a dinner party with wine and cheerful chatter during which, as he later realized, he'd been incredibly bored. The loud, convivial people, the meal, the decor, the customs and rituals, everything that normally belongs to life and gives us pleasure, now led to alienation: they meant nothing to him. This isn't a normal feeling of boredom: it resembles Sartre's nausea, which shows that nothing is actually worthwhile. Similarly, a normal feeling of fear can be distinguished from a deeper-seated fear, one that is linked to existence itself, a fear that casts doubts on your particular existence.

Depression is like that too, something much bigger that targets the foundation of your existence. Grief, worries, tiredness, not looking forward to a particular day or week can occasionally happen to everyone. Such feelings can also be caused by depression, but the depression itself goes deeper and lasts longer. It affects the basic structures of your existence: your relationship with the world (by which I mean relationships with others, with work, with everything that gives your life meaning and purpose); the relationship with the self (depressed people no longer automatically cohere with their own selves, and fall prey to destructive thinking); and the relationship you have with time, and especially with the future.

EVA MEIJER

Becoming an island

In *The Beast and the Sovereign*, by the French philosopher
Jacques Derrida, the fundamental loneliness of human
beings is a central theme.[39] Derrida approaches his subject,
in this his last series of seminars, as always, by a circuitous
route. He discusses the concept of power in Heidegger's
work, in particular the supposed sovereignty, or 'sovereign
domination', of human beings, and also keeps returning to
Robinson Crusoe on his island—simultaneously sovereign
and at the mercy of circumstances. We are all islands,
Derrida writes, we all have our own particular world and
at the same time we share a world with others, the planet
Earth. Our sovereignty seems great, but we are mortal,
and this, moreover, is something we share with the other
animals.

Generally speaking, you do sense or know that we are
all separate from each other, because we can't fully get
under each other's skin, and can never completely adopt
or grasp someone else's point of view, or body, or life.
At the same time, however, you are always with others,
automatically, without even having to consider it. You
are linked to those who are close to you, your colleagues
or classmates, your family and friends; you are rooted in
a social context that you take for granted—even when it
involves a lot of friction. You chat to a colleague, make

jokes with your neighbour, text your sister, call your lover, cuddle your cat. All these interactions form a layer around you that shields you from loneliness, and by that I don't mean feeling alone, but the more fundamental existential awareness that we are all really alone. Depression doesn't only deprive you of your need to connect with others (which you normally do without even thinking about it), it also makes it impossible to spin the strands that will reach them. When you look around you, you see only what separates you from others, not what you share with them.

When you become depressed, you can no longer be roused by the things you enjoy doing, you don't feel like going out any more and taking part in activities, and not only do your relationships with those close to you become difficult to maintain, you no longer care about maintaining them. Sometimes that happens gradually; sometimes at one fell swoop. One of the first things I lose when I become depressed is the ability to make contact with people. The world is still there for a while and animals can console me. But at that point other people affect the distance that I need (to put myself in perspective). If they're emotionally involved with me, then I can't let them see my real state, and I have to shield myself. That demands an energy I don't have at that point, and makes me feel even emptier and more alone. If they're more distant, I'm less bothered.

This development is self-reinforcing. If you don't feel connected to other people, see yourself as a burden, and can't bridge the space between yourself and everyone else (who still live in the normal world, where things are warm and colourful, where people sit at the fireside with a glass of wine or chocolate soya milk), you'll start avoiding contact with others. Friends and family members might well be loyal, but after a while the social framework will become more fragile and the interactions less frequent, making the depressed person feel that the distance is even greater, making them keep others even further distant, and so on. You can tell others that you can't bridge the distance, but you can't reduce it when you're depressed.

There is a lesson in this too for those who have to deal with someone close to them who is depressed: know that you can't solve it for them, or make it better. All you can do is be there, helping with practical things such as running the home, and bringing in other help if necessary (from a doctor, psychologist or psychiatrist), or you can take them out for a walk. Don't react with anger or disappointment if things don't improve, your intervention doesn't help, or someone doesn't thank you properly. Don't focus on your worries about the situation, and take care of yourself too, making sure there are plenty of other things you can still enjoy. Keep calm: it could pass. One day it will pass—there is hope, even if someone can't see that for themselves. (And for those who are less involved: perhaps you can help, but probably not. The lines that connect you to that person won't vanish; at the most they have temporarily faded away. It's not about you and it's not your fault. And it's never a bad idea to send a card.)

The empty present

We usually live in three time dimensions at once. The future gives us direction—shopping for the evening meal, making a promise to someone, or planning to write a book. The past gives us form: this was like that then and now it's like this—memories help us to understand the here and now, a certain feeling is like an earlier feeling and I am who I was, evolving. The present holds us and gives us now to walk on, step by step. This is how we are able to move forward. The depressed person, however, is cut off from her present; it has expired. Activities no longer seem to have any purpose; everyday needs can hardly be fulfilled. She is also cut off from her past because who she was is no longer really who she is, and because what she once loved no longer seems important. But perhaps the most important thing is that

47

she's also cut off from the future. Since nothing is worth doing, there's nothing to live for. During a depression you understand how important it is to be able to look forward to something.

The dimensions of time run together too. The future transforms into a kind of repetitive now: if you're lucky you can perceive the extent of a day, but more often it's about surviving the moments. The past turns into a strange fiction, more distant than usual—once things were good, but it's impossible to understand how; a bare kind of knowing, without actually feeling it. During a depression you are presented with a new map of your life: what happened in the past is displayed again, but now in the context of depression. Events have a tendency to be coloured by memory, but the reverse also happens: memories take on the colour of your mood at a particular moment. The past isn't fixed, it just stalks you (and like a good stalker it often changes disguise). Despair points to previous despair, which strengthens it, just as grief draws other, older griefs to the surface. Events from the past can suddenly be summoned into the foreground—and during a depression these are always the bad things, never the good ones.

What remains is an empty present. We can no longer orientate ourselves in time. Andrew Solomon describes depression as a kind of timelessness, in which past and future are completely dominated by this lost present. You can't imagine any future that could be better; at the most you can vaguely remember better times in the past. This is one of the big differences between depression and grief. Grief often leaves the past intact, although the future is damaged.

The empty you

Besides needing a future, you also need trust to be able to live. You need it for all kinds of things, big and small. To build a real relationship, you need to trust that the one you love also loves you; to find meaning in your work, you need to feel that it's worthwhile; to use the roads, you have to believe that your fellow road-users will obey the traffic regulations. If your basic trust in yourself and in the world is lost, along with the hope that things will one day improve, it becomes almost impossible to move. If someone you love has ever bamboozled you, you know how difficult it is to trust a loved one again. Losing confidence in yourself is just as drastic. You need yourself for almost everything. The empty husk into which your body has changed can still be controlled, perhaps, during a depression, but why would you bother? It's also strange that others still perceive you as a human being, that the darkness that has swallowed you up has left your body undamaged.

Too sad to tell you

People often imagine that great sorrow and terrible pain produce extreme manifestations of emotion (although this differs between cultures): the deeper the sorrow, the more intense the external reaction. Although there are depressed people who cry constantly, whose tears flow for the slightest or most trivial things, there are also many who are taken over by silence. I belong to the latter category— sometimes when I'm merely sad, and certainly when I'm depressed. My body language flattens, my voice grows softer, I react less. This can be compared to the way that coldness makes your skin feel tight; it feels like something that comes from the outside and attaches itself to me. If I do cry, it brings no relief, simply exhaustion—and a feeling of endlessness.

Perhaps the sadness hasn't gone, but is too deep. In *I'm Too Sad to Tell You*, a silent film by the Dutch conceptual artist Bas Jan Ader, you see his face in close-up.[40] Ader rubs a hand over his eyes and cheeks and through his hair, seeming to provoke the tears, which soon start flowing. His expression is tormented and at the same time it's almost abstract—it's not a reality TV show, in which people shed tears for the kinds of things that all of us can cry about (a dog that's been rescued, people finding each other again, against all the odds; it's always about love or (escaping) death), but Ader's grief is a stylized sorrow with an unknown cause. Precisely because we don't know what Ader is sad about, his sorrow gains a universal value. Yet Ader was criticized for the surface nature of the film, for its kitschiness even. Ader's sincerity has been doubted—it isn't clear whether he is really sad or simply stirring up the tears and acting out the emotion.[41] This reading isn't convincing, however, precisely because of the stylized nature of the emotion—the film abstracts the experience, thereby making it artificial. The intensity of his grimaces does suggest deep feelings, but those feelings aren't revealed to us because we lack the story behind them.

Depressions often come for no reason. The depressed person doesn't understand why they feel like this and the outside world doesn't understand it either—hey, it's spring again, you have the whole of your life ahead of you, you're so smart and so good. Ader reveals the distance between the one and the other, separated by an incomprehensible, wordless feeling, and he also shows its strangeness and depth.

The waves

Unlike the memoir-writers I mentioned previously, Ader doesn't use words to display his, or rather, a general suffering. The beauty and difficulty of language is that you can never say exactly what you want to say: you always say both more and less. Less because a word, as Wittgenstein says, is a signpost (and not the thing pointed to); more because language takes us beyond the individual—words always include all kinds of cultural and social connotations—and they can sketch a new world.

Memoirs about depression are often limited in their use of language: the big story they're telling is foregrounded—their goal is to create an emotional response, to show us how bad it all is. Sex sells, but pain sells just as well; plenty of readers enjoy being disaster tourists. I don't want to suggest that these memoirs serve no purpose: by carefully describing the course of their depression, such writers offer an insight into the grimness of their thoughts and give some kind of background to actions that would otherwise be incomprehensible. Yet the language itself does not play a part in this; it is used only instrumentally.

But there are writers who show what happens in depression precisely through their use of words. One of the finest examples of this is Virginia Woolf's *The Waves*. Although *The Waves* is not a novel about depression—and there's a greater sense of resignation in *Jacob's Room*, *To the Lighthouse* or even *Mrs Dalloway*—the characters contend with time, which slips through their hands like a smooth rope, with the loss of dreams and loved ones, and with the disappointment of fulfilled and unfulfilled desires. That is the material from which depression is partly made. Woolf's characters nearly always have a deep awareness of the evanescence and desolateness of things: the women, in particular, are frequently bound to a world in which they cannot flourish. In *The Waves* the language follows the fragmentation of experience—or experience follows the language. The book starts in darkness: 'The sun had not yet risen.' The sea is only distinguishable from the sky because of its waves, which are like little wrinkles on cloth. In the very last sentence the waves break on the shore (they keep on breaking, without ever getting broken). In between, the lives of humans move like waves, back and forth, with fragments of thoughts and conversation coming up above the water and then vanishing again. Everything passes, everything constantly begins anew. The book doesn't give us a rounded story, or the facts about depression or the meaninglessness of life. It conveys a mood that breaks over the reader, if the reader invests time in it.[42]

The shape you acquire

People weather over the course of their lives, and depressions colour that process. They tinge you, and partially shape you. What you learn from a depression is that the dark things that normally seem far distant are actually inside you. We already carry the darkness with us. Death is inside your body, and in time, in which you live; we are temporal beings, after all. Endings seem far away until they're suddenly there—you understand that when someone you love dies, or if a lover leaves you. Depression wraps you up inside those endings, and thereby freezes time. What normally shields us from the fact that everything vanishes are the connections we make with others (friends, lovers, animals), our plans for the future, the feeling that in spite of everything there are things that are worthwhile. If these things vanish in the way I described above, then all that is left is a barren landscape where you can't actually live.

The truths of the depressed person and the one who isn't depressed are equally true. There are things that are worthwhile; everything does pass, vanishing into the void from which it came. The harsh awareness of the latter is almost unbearable, but it can also put more superficial concerns into perspective. And when the worst is over and a few plants grow again among the rocks, and there are some animals living too, and maybe there's even someone who sometimes holds your hand, then the insights from your depression can help you get your bearings. If you've gone through a period of depression, you know it's a waste to spend time on things that aren't actually worthwhile—superficial things, except if you really love them, as some people love clothes or food; or things that are false. At any rate, it grants me a pleasant distance from things many people seem to worry about, such as outward appearance, making money, or pretending to be better than you are. The things that are really important gain more weight: because you had to work hard for them, because things do matter once again.

Although everything has been going well for some time now, I still consider myself to be someone susceptible to depression. Fragments of it still recur every now and then (or are they simply a part of who I am?). I can easily feel estranged from myself and from my life, and at night there is sometimes a lurking, background fear that gets into my dreams, wakes me up, keeps me awake. It's a fear of what is inevitable: that the dogs will die, that my parents will die; ultimately, far too generalized a feeling to fight against with arguments or other thoughts. This world will end, I'm lying here now and everything is already ending.

Sometimes it's twilight, then I'm under a shadow or a soft black layer, as if a wash of watercolour has been painted across me and everything else. I'm not standing in the light then, nor in darkness; I can see both. I know it could be better than this, but something's wrong and I have to stay alert. I also know it could be far worse: I can still think, make plans, move. In this phase I make sure to keep running and going outside. If necessary, I put my thoughts in brackets (this is just something I'm thinking, it's not actually the case; it doesn't matter what I think, just keep going) and I accept that there are wasted days, days that weren't worthwhile. They'll pass, and there will be new ones.

I know I'll become depressed again, one day—unless I'm very lucky, but I wouldn't count on that. If something bad happens, I keep a close eye on my own state of mind, as if I'm a doctor. What am I feeling now? Who or what is this pain about? What colour is the sky? Am I seeing in colour? How long haven't I been? If I wake up with a vague tummy ache (one that is clearly different from something with a physical cause), I do the same: what am I thinking, how can I shake this off, or what is the most comfortable way to bear it? An important aspect of getting used to life and to yourself, of course, is learning how you can best bear things. People underestimate how much you have to get used to life, forget that for many people life isn't something they can do right away, that some never learn.

As well as these kinds of everyday practical consid-
erations, my susceptibility to depression also influences
the way I think about the future. For a long time I didn't
want to have children because I wanted to reserve the
right to put an end to my life. There have been plenty
of days when the only comfort was that I could just stop.
Now that I'm not depressed this seems over-the-top and
dramatic, but there's a part of me that is still bothered by
the preconception that if you can speak and write about
what's happening to you, you can eventually overcome
it. This is really not the case. Depression is a sneaking,
slumbering, and sometimes all-encompassing feeling that
could theoretically kill me. I have thrown out anchors of
every kind, I've built dams, and I'm pretty safe here, but
I still know that things could go wrong– and knowing that
has become a part of how I understand myself and my
life. This may not be as bad as it seems. To keep someone
alive who is persistently and repeatedly depressed could
be far worse.

In his *Letters on Ethics* Seneca displays a rather laconic
attitude to death.[43] The important thing, he says, is not to
live, but to live well. Life is a performance and what matters
is not how long it lasts, but how virtuous it is. Dying isn't
something bad: we came from nothing and will return to
nothing. Not being born doesn't hurt anyone and so you
don't have to be afraid that dying will harm you. He adds

that death is preferable to a bad life. Even stronger: we shouldn't complain about life, because no one is keeping us there. Are we suffering from an illness that will pass? Then we should resign ourselves to it (and depressions usually do pass, don't forget, although it may not seem so and the days during a depression are far too long). But if we have no chance of recovery, we should take matters into our own hands and seek death. He gives examples of people who, even in the most difficult circumstances, managed to choose death—such as a slave who put his head between the spokes of a chariot wheel and so broke his neck, and a wild-beast gladiator who choked himself to death by stuffing a sponge on a stick down his throat. It is difficult to live as Seneca proposes, because as human beings we attach ourselves to everything. We have to form attachments, because that is a part of living well, and it's important to invest in that. But that death is a part of life, and that there are worse things than death, is something Seneca is right about. 'No journey is without a destination,' he adds cheerfully.

3

On healing and the benefits of madness

A rotatory swing is made by fixing a shaft to both the floor and the ceiling and attaching a simple rotating system onto it. The melancholic sits on a chair or couch fixed to the shaft and is tied in tightly with a straitjacket. Then he or she is spun around at an increasing speed; if this makes the patient manic, an interrupted rhythm can be used. According to the physician Joseph Mason Cox (1763–1818),[44] this method was very effective for combatting melancholy. In the late eighteenth and early nineteenth centuries, the swing was used in various places to cure melancholics.[45] The body was the focus for treating the symptoms; the illness was not yet purely perceived as a disease of the mind.[46] In addition to the use of the rotatory swing, music was thought to be helpful, as well as stage plays, performed for the insane, or in which they were forced to participate. The inducement of fear was also an accepted form of treatment.

Lurking behind these methods were ideas about the 'animal spirits' of human beings, which in melancholy were dark and sombre. The world of melancholia was heavy and cold, a way of thinking about it that derives from the work of Hippocrates, who thought that the temperament of human beings was determined by four bodily humours: blood, phlegm, black bile and yellow bile. People could be classified into different types according to the balance of their humours: a surplus of blood made someone spirited and energetic, or of a sanguine nature; too much phlegm made them phlegmatic; too much yellow bile made them easily irritated, or bilious; and too much black bile made them melancholic, or atrabilious. Galen, a second-century Greco-Roman physician, linked these humours to heat, cold, damp, and dryness—a surplus of black bile led to cold and dryness. It wasn't until the mid-nineteenth century that these ideas about the human temperaments were refuted.

In *Madness and Civilization*, Michel Foucault shows how people started to think differently about mental illnesses in the prelude to the modern era. In pre-modern times, melancholy was regarded as part of the spectrum of human experience, as were other mental deviations; it wasn't necessarily perceived as something irrational. In the modern age, however, madness came to be opposed to reason, and melancholy was situated in the patient's head.

Therapy proceeds from the ideas that people have about madness, and is subject to fashions, as the previous examples show. Virginia Woolf had three teeth pulled out to cure her depressions, something she later regretted when the treatment didn't help. I grew up in a society that sees therapy, in the form of talking and medication, as the answer to problems that trouble the mind. The girls' magazines of my youth were full of sad but also optimistic and informative articles and personal stories about anorexia, borderline personality disorder, and other conditions. They stressed that these conditions could be cured and that the best thing was to talk about your problems and seek help. For physical symptoms you visit the doctor; for psychological complaints you go to the Regional Institute for Outpatient Mental Health Care.

During the depression that started when I was fourteen, I became more and more lost. The illness ate into my thoughts, leaving only a feeling of worthlessness in the gaps. So I reported to the Regional Institute, where every fortnight a friendly lady, with the air of a washed-out dishcloth, let me talk for three quarters of an hour about my afflictions, without me having any idea where it was leading, and without me feeling one jot better. I don't think

61

she knew or understood how I felt, and these conversations made me feel more rather than less isolated.

My state slowly worsened. I drank a lot and went out almost every evening. I increasingly skipped school, for the simple reason that I couldn't sit in a classroom all day. I also started eating less. That seemed like a good way to punish myself and to gain control of the feeling that was engulfing me. It worked pretty well at first. I felt less, and my thoughts had found a focus. I was constantly checking my body, weighing it and measuring the clasp of my fingers around my wrists and thighs.

Losing weight can start as a conscious choice, but somewhere en route, when you're really underweight, the balance tips and weight loss controls you. Depression takes over your thoughts and colours your environment, but for me it carried and still carries a certain existential truth (life really is unbearable sometimes), even though it includes ideas that aren't correct, that you could certainly call 'crazy'. The eating disorder, on the other hand, dictated things to me that I knew weren't true, but I still had to act on them. I knew very well that I was thin, too thin, increasingly thin, and yet I wasn't thin enough. I knew very well that I had just as much right to exist as others, and yet I didn't have that right. I knew very well that I was slowly and unnecessarily dying, and yet it was necessary.

By 'crazy' I mean roughly the following: the world that others see, and in which they live, is still there, but it is no longer mine. The space between that world and my own experience demonstrates my madness. Not my experience itself—that's just there. But because it doesn't cohere with what I know is actually true, measured by what other people think and what I myself would think if I weren't mad, I know that it's madness.

An element of this is that I have thoughts that aren't really mine any more, and which I'm also able to criticize, sometimes even while thinking them, intertwined with a feeling that can range from fear to deep gloom, whose intensity makes normal movement impossible. An example is the thought: I have to die. I know there's no reason why that should be so, I even know that I don't have to die, and yet it really is so. In terms of how it feels, a panic attack is a good example: there's no big predator chasing you and you're not falling into an abyss, and yet you're over-alert: your stomach feels as if you're falling, your breathing is too fast, your skin is prickling, the panic rises up from your diaphragm. Such an attack is a storm that catches you unawares, which you have to sit out, but it has nothing at all to do with survival. It's a surplus, madness, an unnecessary experience that plucks you out of the world, only to drop you back into it again later—all you are is a body that can simply be picked up, so it's better to give way a little.

Madness can be compared to falling in love (in the seventeenth century lovesickness was regarded as a manifestation of madness). When you fall in love, you're also taken over by something that is actually quite alien. You gain a world, the world that belongs to the other, and lose a world—your own world, as it was before. Your thoughts and feelings have been hijacked, they're no longer familiar to you, and are difficult or impossible to steer, they keep returning of their own accord to the object of your affection. Someone from the periphery of your life is suddenly the centre that irresistibly draws you. You can yield, or struggle against it, but you can't think the feeling away, although if you ignore it long enough, it can often quench itself. Being in love, or being addicted to drugs, is of course different to madness, because it's focused on someone or something outside yourself, but it does show how in various ways we can't be in charge.

Madness means you can't trust yourself. We can only be our own compass, and if that is constantly spinning, you end up getting further and further from your destination, whichever way you walk.

In his book *A Philosophy of Madness*[47] Wouter Kusters fights for the need to think differently about being mad. He uses the term 'madness' to refer specifically to episodes of psychosis, which he perceives as an expansion, rather than a deviation or a narrowing of consciousness. A psychosis calls into question the reality that most people experience, effectively turning it upside down, but to write that off as being inferior, as is prevalent in psychiatric discourse, means that its wisdom and richness aren't perceived. Kusters is certainly not saying that it's perfectly all right to be psychotic, simply that it's an experience that affords its own insights about the human condition. He describes the last psychotic episode he had as a personal disaster, but a blessing for the book.

Psychosis, according to Kusters, turns the reality of the psychotic person around in such a way that it seems the world has changed, and not the person. During a depression, the world is also unrecognizable, but in a different way. The depressed person turns inwards, while someone suffering from psychosis becomes over-concerned with the outside world (because of paranoia, for example, or delusions of grandeur). The magical dimension of psychosis is lacking in depression, and the enrichment that Kusters describes, the expansion of the world, which from his point of view can also be experienced with drugs, is in my experience of depression actually a curtailment: everything becomes more barren. The hyperrealism that Kusters describes (and the accompanying alienation) is certainly recognizable, and so is the gap between your experience and that of others. But depression gives you a winter landscape, while in psychosis, at least as Kusters describes it, it's high summer.

Slowly disappearing

And so for a few years I hovered in a world beside the world, controlled by strange rules about walking and cycling and eating the occasional apple. My anorexia wasn't about eating or losing weight: it was an effective way of disappearing. The literal disappearance happened in plain sight. Extreme thinness draws people's attention, making you into a medical case in the eyes of passers-by, while at the same time it's a mask. A body reduced to skin and bones becomes anonymous, its form vanishes, the person inside it becomes a patient. But for me the aim was more about a different kind of disappearance: not-eating reduces almost all experience to thinking about food and the body, and that is an effective distraction from other problems.

In *A Hunger Artist* Kafka writes about someone who has turned the act of not-eating into his profession. The character is very proud of this. He fasts for forty days in every city that he visits—he would even like to carry on longer, but after that the public loses interest. His fasting is checked day and night, often by butchers, strangely enough, as the narrator comments. For him, the most annoying ones are those who sit at night playing cards with their backs turned towards him, so he can secretly eat something, if he wants—they don't believe that he doesn't want to do this. Sometimes he sings, for as long as he is able, but then, according to the hunger artist, his watchers simply think: how clever that he can eat while he's singing. When the fast is over and he can eat again, he does so at a celebratory public meal. He doesn't really want to do this, but his impresario always forces him.

After spending his life touring, the hunger artist joins a circus where he's put in a cage and is allowed to fast for as long as he likes. At first the public still looks at him, although they often quickly move on to the tigers and elephants, but at a certain point they forget about him. In the last scene of the story, even the attendants have forgotten him. When someone wants to clean out the cage and the hunger artist is discovered, he tells the supervisor that he'd really like them to admire him. Then he says that he doesn't want them to admire him. He finally tells them that he simply couldn't find the food he liked, while all pride at being good at fasting has vanished from his eyes. The other people, first the general public and now the circus employees, are indifferent; they really couldn't care less whether he fasts, or even whether he exists. The fasting is an addiction that has reduced the person behind it to a junkie, just as other addictions do. When the hunger artist realizes that there's nothing noble about it, it's too late.

You just can't win, as Kafka shows in this story—fasting is an achievement, but in the long term it devours everything else.[48] Moreover, anorexia is intrinsically extremely boring. You're always doing the same thing and you can never do it well enough.

In the end I hardly slept at all. A body goes into standby mode if it doesn't get enough fuel and lying down really hurts if your spine protrudes too far: it becomes one long bruise. Even lying on a mattress is painful (and the same is true of the bones in your buttocks when you sit).

In *The Book of Disquiet* Pessoa says that the world he enters in his sleep is the real world, and that his everyday waking life is only its pale reflection. The monotony and unhappiness, the pointless goals of daytime, are suffocating, and the only real possibility of escape is in our dreams. These are another world inside this world. When I had anorexia, my dreams—when I finally did sleep—simply duplicated my daily life. I would clench my jaws together in my sleep and make chewing motions; a couple of times I threw up on the pillow—just bile—and then I had eaten something in my dream. A friend of my mother's had an anorexic daughter who once ate her earplugs in her sleep because she was so hungry, and then she threw up because she'd taught her body to react to food like this. There was no possibility of escape, because my body was my dungeon. During the day, my mind still kept the fear under control—mostly, at least, but not always—but at night the slow dying took over. Sometimes I went out in the middle of the night to walk away the panic. The canal was very quiet then: coots bobbed in the reeds by the waterside and ducks lay on the bank, their beaks tucked into their feathers. I just put one foot in front of the other, over and over again, and so the pavement carried me through time.

The night began to seep into the day. I walked and cycled and couldn't stop myself from slipping through my own fingers; I couldn't stop my heart from behaving strangely, or stop my hands and feet from getting bruised, just like my spine. Not existing in an existent body is painful. I was always cold, always hungry. It's a myth that anorexics don't get hungry. I spent a year studying philosophy and music during that time, but I remember very little of it. When I started philosophy again, ten years later, it turned out that I had passed ten modules the first time—all I remembered was that I'd had to repeat one of them; I'd forgotten all the good grades.

It reached a physical low point. I was taking a bath to try and warm up, but I couldn't sit down, it was much too painful, and I suddenly felt, standing there naked in the bathroom, that I was really dying. I cut my arm, and then went to the doctor, who prescribed antidepressants; and in the weeks that followed my parents and I found a good psychologist, who specialized in eating disorders. He told me I would probably have to be admitted to hospital. That seemed like a good idea to me. It's very annoying to have to live with an eating disorder and I didn't want to carry on like that any more—so it was a choice between getting better or being dead.

A few months after my twentieth birthday, I was admitted into a specialist clinic in Leidschendam. My parents and sister brought me there, as if I was going away on a long journey. The car was full of books and clothes and my camera. I also had to bring my own duvet.

The clinic

The clinic was built around a quadrangle and my room looked out onto the inner courtyard. The bed was next to the radiator and under the window. The first few nights I lay in bed, pressed against the radiator, and all I could think was: this is my last chance. I was put into group therapy, in a group of eight people. This kind of therapy was for those with a future, unlike the chronic patients, who were in the individual section on the other side of the clinic.

On the first day I wasn't in therapy yet. I was sent to the medical centre on the other side of the campus with G., another new arrival, whom we later nicknamed the Ghost. G. didn't ask my name, but did ask about my weight. It was a pleasant walk. The clinic belonged to the Rivierduinen Mental Health Care Service and there were several buildings in the grounds, with people with other psychological problems living in some of them, but there was also a sports hall, a dining room and a play farm. The paths were lined with majestic trees. Our building stood in a corner of the grounds, in front of a wet ditch, with meadows behind. They took blood samples in the medical centre and did ECG tests. The two of us walked back together. Twice I had to catch hold of G., because she kept falling.

As well as various kinds of therapy, the treatment involved attempting to put on weight: you had to 'grow' a kilo a week; if you didn't manage that twice, you had to leave. The rule about putting on weight may seem over the top, but if someone is too thin, then therapy is pointless. The person isn't him or herself any more: mind and body are in survival mode. When you're underweight, underlying problems can be rationally discussed, but the emotions are dead. Moreover, established eating patterns need to be changed and for that to happen the anorexic must let go of their control. Any kind of middle way between normal eating and an eating disorder just preserves the trade-offs and calculations. If you have a major eating disorder, it's really not an unnecessary luxury to be admitted into a clinic; it's incredibly difficult to turn around your own eating patterns at home, because of the madness that sets in. In between the various therapies, I'd smoke roll-ups in the courtyard with my fellow patients. Stopping smoking wasn't recommended: that was something I gave up later, when I started singing again.[49] The conversations with my fellow sufferers in that courtyard made it easier to cross the threshold and go back into the world. I could see in them what I was doing and why it didn't make sense. So it can be beneficial to share this form of madness, to know that others are going through the same thing and that they manage to get out. But not everyone succeeds. Around forty-five per cent of the patients recover fully, thirty per cent partially improve, and twenty-five per cent don't get better. Many anorexics are attached to their suffering—it has become part of their identity. Perhaps this is because anorexia is an illness that often starts in puberty, when people are usually learning to express themselves as individuals, and because the illness makes it so difficult for you to build up a life outside it, when, in fact, that's the only way to stop it. There must be something to live for beyond the illness, something to give it up for. Eating disorders are also quite deadly, compared to other mental illnesses. In the Netherlands between five and ten per cent of anorexic patients die, either by suicide or because of their poor physical condition.[50]

Every day in the clinic started with a morning meeting in which everyone spoke about how they were feeling. During the second part of the morning, and in the afternoon, a specific kind of therapy was scheduled: creative therapy, individual psychotherapy, PMT (psychomotor therapy, which is focused on your relationship with your body), sports (swimming or handball) and even group family therapy. We also went on outings: once we went to Amsterdam, another time to the beach, and once even to a café-bar where we drank Caribbean Twist.

For creative therapy, you should imagine a kind of craft room with people working on different assignments, such as creating a collage about the future, using magazine images to compose an ideal body, working on free assignments, or making self-portraits. I made a number of large drawings there which were quite good, but later I put them in my hall cupboard, where I let them get mouldy. The PMT often started with a meditation (bring your attention to your toes, calves, knees) and we also did things like mirroring: standing in front of a mirror with a fellow patient and then looking together at her body or your own body, and describing what you see. Part of the madness of anorexia is a distorted self-image; patients perceive themselves as being much fatter than the norm. That was why video recordings were also made (I remember a scene with golden body paint, but I don't know if that was during creative therapy, or in the PMT sessions). For me the most important therapies, besides the conversations with my fellow group members on the patio or in the smoking room, were cognitive therapy and psychotherapy.

Cognitive behavioural therapy: logic as a tool

Cognitive behavioural therapy focuses on separating positive and negative thoughts. The weeds must, effectively, be pulled from the mind. It starts with making a diagram, composed of three parts: situation, thoughts, and feelings/behaviour. The idea is that each specific situation provokes certain irrational thoughts, from which feelings and behaviour follow. Changing the thoughts will also change the feelings and behaviour. Undesirable thoughts can be challenged in two ways: by questioning their truth value and by showing that they don't work. The thoughts may be something like this: I'm worthless; it's all my fault;

I'm a bad person; it's better for me not to exist. With an eating disorder, there are also things like: I'm fat; I mustn't eat. When you have thoughts of the latter kind, it's good to realize that if you're seriously underweight, they can't be true. With thoughts about badness, it's probably better just to understand that they're not helpful.

CBT techniques were really helpful with regard to the anorexia. (Anorexia is, in fact, a very Cartesian condition: the anorexic sees the body as being separate from the mind, as something that the mind should curb, discipline and control.[51]) The thoughts that accompanied it, about my body and my weight, about being allowed or not allowed to eat, have completely vanished. They continued to haunt me for a while, like spectres, but they eventually gave up: I survived, I trained myself out of it.[52] This way of thinking also helps with depression: being able to put ideas about worthlessness inside brackets is a useful technique for getting through bad times. It also taught me that I'm not always the right person to judge my own worth, which doesn't alter the fact that I'm very self-critical.

The undermining thoughts beneath the eating disorder didn't entirely vanish. Some of those thoughts I consider to be largely untrue (that I'm bad, that everything's my fault) and when they come and visit me again, if I'm tired, or sad, or alone, then I can place them in brackets. Then I'm able to realize that although I may think these things now, this will change: that I'm just tired, or sad, or feeling lonely, and in these circumstances it makes sense to think these kinds of things. The thoughts do not say anything about me, they just say something about how my thinking works. At least, that's the way it normally goes. When both life and thinking get fragmented, become tangled together and spin dark threads round me, this technique doesn't work so well any more. Then I start to sleep badly, and when I sleep badly, I can no longer put things in perspective; then the negative thoughts lodge inside me, translating themselves into my feelings and vice versa; and then a mould begins to grow, first obscuring my joy and then my sense of logic, covering everything, until it's all grey and hazy. When that happens, I switch into a military mode, in which discipline and order are central. (In *The Artist is Present*, her documentary about her life, Marina Abramović describes herself as a soldier—I'm a soldier too). I can and must cancel appointments, because I can't tolerate other people, but I have to go running, walk with the dogs, and work. Sometimes I can't even read any more, and yet I must work. Slowly, then. There's no other option. If I let go of that, I'll slip away.

In that kind of situation, nothing is solved by thinking that my thoughts aren't right, but it does save me time. Putting undesirable thoughts inside brackets leads to an in-between time: in the end you'll have to be able to judge things again. But when everything is getting greyer and greyer, it's already quite an achievement to be able to bracket your thoughts.

This way of dealing with thoughts and reality is related to the academic discipline of philosophy. By critically examining beliefs, philosophers try to discriminate between good ideas and not-so-good ideas, to clarify concepts, and get closer to the truth (often assuming, nowadays, that there is no fixed, ultimate truth, but that there are better and worse arguments). The big difference is that as a philosopher you employ your thinking to understand the world, while in behavioural therapy you learn to distinguish between positive and negative thoughts, or constructive and destructive ones. Cognitive therapy is about the thinkers themselves, not about the world; it isn't primarily focused on truth, but on what works. Pragmatic philosophers do, in fact, think that philosophy works in the same way: we shouldn't try to find out what something is like, because we can never know that anyway, but just how it works.[53]

Dialogue as therapy

What cognitive therapy—and behavioural therapy in general—is less focused on are the stories that form the emotional substratum of our thoughts and behaviour, that maintain them and can even change them. This is exactly what psychotherapy deals with.[54] The events, histories and narratives stored in the body tug at the mind and always form an element of it: we understand what we do and why against that background. The training of behaviour and thinking is very useful, for both humans and other animals, but we are also situated beings who long for understanding and significance.

Sigmund Freud was one of the first to point out the importance of narrative significance in psychotherapy. In his short paper 'Mourning and Melancholia' (1917) he discusses the difference between the two conditions—the latter being more or less the same as what we now call depression. In Freud's opinion, both melancholia and mourning are forms of profound psychic suffering that are based on an experience of loss.[55] Mourning, however, is seen as a normal reaction to specific events, while melancholy is regarded as pathological. By comparing them, Freud tries to grasp what melancholy actually is, as a basis for its treatment.

According to Freud, mourning and melancholy share the following characteristics: a profound dejection, a loss of interest in the outside world, a loss of the ability to love, and the inhibiting of all activity. In the case of melancholy he adds a poor self-image and the expectation of punishment. Mourning is caused by the loss of a concrete object: a loved one, an idea, or something else. Melancholy is also characterized by loss, but it is unclear what exactly was lost. This loss leads to the erasure of a part of one's identity, and finds expression in a death wish and a poor self-image. (That poor self-image, Freud says, is in fact always undeserved, and strangely enough it is often the most capable people who feel that way, and not those who really should doubt themselves.) In cases of mourning the world becomes empty, whereas in melancholia it is the ego. Freud's explanation for this is that the melancholic has probably also suffered the loss of something that was loved, but in this case the loss has turned inwards. This causes a withdrawal of the libido into the ego, a movement of the lost object into the ego itself. So instead of going through a process of mourning and severing the ties with the lost object, to make room for the new reality, the ego identifies with the loss, which solidifies in that identification. This is a narcissistic movement and leads to the loss of ego that characterizes melancholy.

Freud thought that as humans we are largely driven by our subconscious, by drives that we curb by means of the ego. When events that have occurred in childhood are suppressed, this can lead to problems; in psychoanalysis, therefore, the patient and the therapist together try to discover the disturbing events that have made the patient who she is. The sessions are frequent and it is mainly the patient who speaks, with her dreams also forming a subject of discussion. Freud's ideas have been criticized from various angles. His method has been perceived as insufficiently scientific, for example (because the effects of the therapy cannot be objectively measured, although there are plenty of people who say they have benefited from it), because the relationship between the therapist and patient is thought to be too authoritarian, and because the whole idea of the unconscious is seen as a fable. But even if this were the case, it doesn't diminish the fact that Freud is a good writer and that his work is still worth reading. He is a powerful storyteller and has profoundly influenced our thinking about the psyche, by bringing in the concept of the subconscious, for example. Moreover, the idea of using dialogue as a way of helping someone to get better is one of great beauty.

To understand therapy as a dialogue does justice to the role that language plays in our conception of our environment and ourselves. The relationship between experience and reality is generally represented as follows. Our experience is strictly personal and individual, but we can convey it to others by means of words. The words we use point to things around us: objects, emotions, relationships, and so on. But that is a misleading picture. I can use words to sketch a map of my feelings for you, but those words are not the same as the feeling. They never completely coincide with what is happening—they're not a horse, but an image of a horse, and at the same time they give us the possibility of describing that horse again, on the basis of her scent, the soft hair on her nose, other earlier horses, the colour of her coat, the way she raises her head and looks at you. All the thousands of little pieces show something. Each reader or listener links them together in their own way. Language can bridge the distance to the other and at the same time it separates us from them—just as our skin does. Those with more words at their disposal don't necessarily have a richer emotional life than others (music is as rich as language; different languages offer different forms of expression; and many animals have languages without words), but they may possess a richer palette to interpret that emotional life and give it meaning.

In his *Philosophical Investigations* Wittgenstein says that although mental experiences may be private, language is always necessarily public. It is impossible to speak of a private language. Language is, therefore, not only a framework for describing your experiences to others, but is also a grid within which you shape those experiences for yourself. Although we can think in music and images, the way that an event or an image is made concrete always takes place in the words you learnt as a child. In

'The World is a Word'[56] Patricia De Martelaere says that this is why we always see the world through the words of others, that is, via the culture that already existed. Words don't literally point to things; because of their cultural dimension they also make them. To see a tree as a tree classifies a whole category of plants, which could, in fact, be structured differently.

Talking about events and feelings is much more, therefore, than simply digging things up or looking them in the eye: it can reshape what has already happened. And dialogue, of course, is a tried and tested philosophical method: Socrates was already searching for truth through his discussions with others. In the context of healing, however, I don't know if therapists and patients always search for truth; or rather, I don't think that the truth is always a necessary ingredient in the healing process. In behavioural therapy, for example, it's more important to proceed on the basis of thoughts that work rather than investigating if these are completely true. But in talking therapy searching for the truth does play a role. Not in the sense of discovering the truth or laying it bare, like a detective, as if there's a script ready and waiting, but in the sense of working out what is actually going on, which past it fits into, the twists and turns your thoughts have taken, and then sometimes straightening them out, and sometimes letting them fan out.

I don't mean to imply that there's a fixed true self that has to be reclaimed. Courses in spirituality sometimes advertise themselves with slogans such as 'In Search of Your Self' or 'Find Your Self', something that is based on the idea of a lost authentic core. Of course, countless people do live their lives in various degrees of unhappiness, because they're stuck in relationships, work, or other patterns that aren't good for them, so that time, thinking things over, or being out of doors, can lead to improvements. But the idea of an authentic self that can be unearthed via rebirthing or tantric exercises is romantic and old-fashioned, and actually static in nature. We are always in motion and that we can understand ourselves anew, understand ourselves differently, and thereby change, is of the greatest importance for any kind of growth whatsoever. (And it's also important to make sure not to become some kind of spiritual fortune seeker. There are people who think their unhappiness can be annulled and that they'll finally become who they really are if only they could find the right therapy. Yet unhappiness is a part of life, while therapy can also turn into an addiction and is often an expression of consumerism.) No one has a right to happiness, no one can force it; the question is whether it's even worth pursuing.

I've had talking therapy with a number of different therapists—from the age of fourteen to the age of twenty-one and then once again later—and at a certain point I did know where specific thoughts came from. This map keeps shifting under the influence of new events, but I can rise above it and look at my behaviour from a distar e (which is why it's good for everyone to have thera y at some point). Talking can give relief, it can reshape memories, and adjust the self and its thoughts, but it is not a medicine that will last for ever, it isn't a panacea; it may be necessary again, and sometimes it doesn't help at all. Thinking is not a machine that can be mended. Understanding doesn't always lead to change; certain traits and tendencies can prove to be stubborn.

Even normal talking to others isn't always an option for people with mental troubles, although it's often mentioned as being important and as something to aim for. When you're depressed, you have to work really hard just to keep your footing, and talking to friends or family can make things worse, because you then have to respond to their sadness, fear, worries and disbelief (and disbelief is the easiest to respond to). And sometimes it's literally not possible to talk because the words aren't there, because depression cuts you off from the rest of the world and makes everything dead and cold. When you're in despair, it's important to tackle that, to start working on it with medication, and so forth. But to share what you're going through isn't always possible; we can't expect that of each other, or of ourselves.

Medicines and social justice

I never thought I'd reach the age of eighteen, but time passes of its own accord, and that milestone made me even unhappier than I already was. The doctor I consulted as a result of this came up with the idea of prescribing me an antidepressant (paroxetine, also known as Seroxat).[57] At first, I didn't notice much effect. When things were bad I kept using it, because things were bad; when things went better I used it because I was scared that if I stopped, it would all get worse again. When I turned twenty-four, everything had been going well for quite a while, and so I stopped taking it. For a few months, I was dizzy and nauseous, but mainly I felt more like myself. A new self, because I wasn't a child any more. I fell in love, then fell in love again, and I played the piano constantly, because that allowed me to express what I was feeling better than anything else. The medication certainly helped me find my place in the world, but perhaps I could have followed the same route without it. What I do know is that colours became stronger and that I felt more and wanted more once I stopped. And I regained my fighting spirit. Filing the edges of the darkness had apparently also filed off my pugnacity.

Antidepressants and other psychiatric drugs can contain and correct the chemical madness. For many people they are lifesavers.[58] However, they don't work for everyone and can have severe side effects. In the Netherlands in 2017 more than a million people were on antidepressants.[59] That's a lot of people and there has also been a lot of discussion about it. There are psychiatrists who argue that these kinds of medicines are too easily prescribed, while others specifically favour their use. A recent large-scale study in the UK of more than 116,000 people demonstrates that antidepressants do work.[60] Not for everyone, not always, but they do save lives. Those who have never experienced depression can't perhaps imagine the feeling of relief when you sense that the fog is lifting. But depression can literally paralyse you and for some people chemicals can get rid of that paralysis.

This is not to say that pills are a miracle cure. In *Depression: A Public Feeling* Ann Cvetkovich investigates the sociocultural dimensions of depression.[61] Although they can help individual people, Cvetkovich thinks that pills aren't a solution for depression, because aspects of our culture—such as racism, colonialism, neoliberalism and capitalism—help to create depression amongst specific groups. Sometimes it's easy to see that connection. If you're part of a minority that is perceived by the majority as being inferior, you can start internalizing that image of yourself. This is the case, for example, for queer teenagers, who suffer more from depression than their peers and who commit suicide much more frequently,[62] and recent studies have shown that black people are similarly affected, both in New York[63] and in the UK.[64] Depression and feelings of inferiority can also be passed down through the generations, even at the genetic level[65]. This means that the second-generation victims of major cultural traumas can be born with psychological baggage, quite apart from what they learn about fear, feeling safe, or belonging. According to a study published in 2013, Afghanistan had the highest worldwide level of depression per head of population, closely followed by other countries in the Middle East and North Africa.[66] Depression can also affect specific groups of people who help other groups. Animal rights activists, confronted day after day with the suffering of nonhuman animals, can develop compassion fatigue,[67] while in the US veterinary surgeons have one and a half times more likelihood of getting depressed and are three times more likely to feel suicidal than the rest of the population.[68] Although depression colours individual experience, in thinking about cures, it's important to look beyond the individual.

According to Cvetkovich, our emphasis on medicalizing depression, and on making an individual better, camouflages the cultural and social processes that lead to illness,[69] and medication is often no more than a bandage to staunch the bleeding. As far as she is concerned, such large groups of people aren't unhappy without a reason.[70] If we want to think about making structural improvements, we should at least look at these processes. Moreover, there are groups for whom the western, individualistic approach to curing depression doesn't work well. This is because this model takes as its starting point a specific sort of human being, a kind of atomistic consumer, and then presents that consumer with an ideal image, to be attained by popping pills. This ignores the fact that people are more than consumers and always stand in relation to others. It also ignores cultural differences. It's right, therefore, to look critically at our image of what we think of as being mad and what as healthy.

Better?

In *Madness and Civilization* Foucault, who himself became depressed as a twenty-year-old student, shows how our concept of madness—and the opposite idea, that of normality or rationality—came into being. This concept isn't based on biological reality: it is a cultural phenomenon, shaped by all kinds of historical processes. As I have already discussed, in Ancient Greece, and long after, the origins of madness were thought to lie in an incorrect balance of the four bodily humours; an excess of black bile was seen as leading to dejection. In the Middle Ages demons who settled in the human soul were added to the concept. Then for a while, in the Renaissance era, melancholia became fashionable, especially in England, as reflected in the art, music and literature of the period. Throughout all these periods, madness was perceived as an aspect of human experience that could tell us something about the human condition. In the Enlightenment, however, reason came to be central to our thinking about human beings. Madness was set against reason: you couldn't be both mad and rational at the same time.[71] Reason was viewed as a purely human capacity and developing it was seen as something we should all strive for—those that couldn't do so, the irrational ones, came to be regarded as inferior. Foucault points out that the opposition between madness and reason is of relatively recent origin and wonders whether madness really is something that should be eradicated.

Foucault's method is genealogical: he investigates the meaning of a concept by teasing out its history. In *Madness and Civilization* he searches for the point in history at which reason and madness were not yet separated. He locates the break between these concepts at the end of the eighteenth century and describes what led to it. This journey takes us past ships of fools that transported the insane to other cities,[72] cages in which they were locked up, circuses and zoos where they were put on show,[73] and places where they were used as beasts of burden, to the hospitals and clinics of today. Foucault does not wish to discuss madness in the language of psychiatry, but to give words to the silence that opposes it. This is why he calls his investigation archaeological. What has been handed down to us are mainly the words of the doctors, institutions, and politicians, and not those of the mad people themselves.[74] To allow them to speak at last, we have to search for what remains.

These remains can be found, for example, in texts, buildings and artefacts, and they show us that the concept of madness has always been changing. In various different eras it was viewed as an element of the human soul, a surplus of a specific physical substance, a problem involving our animal spirits, a religious question, a bodily illness, and finally as a mental illness. In the Netherlands, the insane are no longer locked up in dungeons and cages, but our approach to madness isn't neutral. A norm has developed in the course of time, that of the mentally healthy person, and those who deviate from that norm are perceived as having less value—we have to cure them. There is a power relationship at play in clinics, just as in prisons or in schools, one aimed at moulding the mind. This again relates to policy; madness is not simply a medical category, but a political and social one too. Economic forces also play a role here. The pharmaceutical industry, for instance, has power over people's lives by making certain medicines available or not, or by making them so expensive that many people can't afford them. Policymakers want people to be drawn into a particular system because then they will cost less.

The critical method that Foucault employs challenges our image of madness and health, and that challenge raises the question as to what getting better actually means. As I discussed earlier, in *The Philosophy of Madness* Wouter Kusters says that psychoses show us something different about reality than standard experiences, and that this makes them valuable. The language of psychiatry disguises this, because it frames everything as sickness and cure, normal and abnormal (and writers should always question the language). Similarly, depression can show us things that lie beneath the surface—about ourselves, others, the world, and what is and isn't worthwhile. The perspective that depression offers may be one-sided—for the depressed person it only seems possible to look at the world with deep despondency, although there are other

ways of seeing it, which will hopefully return; but thinking and writing about depression can lead to insight, and
sometimes this produces art.

The benefits of madness

Part of what we perceive as madness is perhaps not so very
mad at all. Life is actually very difficult: we're flung into
it as bodies that can break down in all sorts of ways, and
the fact that we lose others is hard to stomach. It really
isn't so peculiar to find this problematic, or to handle it
differently than other people, by shaping it into art, for
example, or by expressing yourself in a way that differs from
the norm. Nearly all people, and many other animals too,
have had to deal with madness at some point in their lives,
whether this takes the form of anxiety attacks, a deep grief
that temporarily deprives life of its meaning, periods of
depression, or delusions. Most people may skim past these
things, just about managing to stay this side of normal.
But those boundaries are not as hard and fast as many
people think, and being strange also has its advantages.[75]

Outsiders are essential for a healthy society. The out-
sider is also an important literary figure, because those
who come from outside cast a different light on what was

already there.[76] A king needs a fool; a society needs people who think differently. People who experience the world and life in a different way are able to question what others see as normal or don't even notice. A Swedish study that investigated the relationship between madness and artistry shows a clear link between creativity and mood disorders.[77] More than a million people were investigated and it was apparent that those with creative professions, such as visual artists, dancers, photographers and writers, were eight per cent more likely to have a bipolar disorder. The specific chances for writers were even higher, with twelve per cent more likelihood, and writers, as I previously mentioned, are also fifty per cent more likely to commit suicide than the rest of the population. In general, people who are in creative professions have a higher risk of depression, schizophrenia, bipolar disorders, anorexia and autism, and are often more likely than average to have relatives who suffer from these disorders.

Aristotle believed that people with a melancholic constitution have a richer soul. In the fragment 'Problems XXX.1' he describes a clear relationship between excelling in politics, poetry or philosophy and having a surplus of black bile. Geniuses often suffer from melancholia, he concludes, and madness and genius lie close together.

That melancholy and depression have positive aspects, and that the boundaries between being mad and being healthy are not fixed, is of little comfort to someone dragged down by their weight. Not everyone can be cured and for many people depression has a tendency to return. For some it happens seasonally, as if humans were gardens, blooming and growing bare again in a sequence beyond their control. Fortunately, there are some ways of coping with the cold and drought.

4

On the wisdom of my feet
and the memory-body

In October 2015 I took part in *This Progress*, an art project by Tino Sehgal, at the Stedelijk Museum in Amsterdam. This work takes the visitor on a walk in which she is guided first by a child, then a teenager, then an adult, and finally an older person. The visitor and the guides, or 'interpreters', hold a conversation while they're walking, in which some of the elements are fixed. (I won't give away how it works, but if you ever get the chance to experience it, I can heartily recommend it.) The interpreters in my group had to start each conversation with a question or comment, and I often asked visitors to talk about a scent that defined their childhood, or which was important to them for some other reason. (Someone asked me if I had a memory like that, and for me it's the scent of a horse.) Many people thought that memories were some kind of data, stored in the brain, just as information is stored in a computer. This metaphor can indeed explain some of the properties of memories, but not how they change over time or through new experiences, nor how they're laced into the body and at the same time attached to the outside world. Scents take us back to our grandparents' house, songs to a bright summer evening at a pony camp, and the voice of a loved one can link layers of time together. Memories are much more fluid than data, more tangible too. Perhaps stories are a better metaphor for memories. Stories also change over time, and because of who tells them; stories that people tell themselves and others change with them. And they change us too, whether they're our own stories, or those of others.

In the art project we deliberately walked through the rooms of the museum at a slower pace than usual. Walking slowly had an effect on the conversations and created space; the movement gave the conversations air and progress. The visitors sometimes wanted to walk faster than intended; then it was important to take them along in a rhythm that was unnatural for them. It was that adjustment, in fact, that forced people out of their habits, and made them say a lot about themselves (people blushed, cried, looked aside or straight at you, and some people got angry).

Walking influences thinking. I walk with the dogs each day for at least a couple of hours and run for an hour every other day. This works better for me than antide-pressants. When I stopped using Seroxat, I was nauseous for six weeks, and then a curtain lifted and it was easier to see both the world and myself. The darkness, however, hadn't entirely vanished. I kept it in check by singing and by letting the days pass via a strict routine. Pika, the dog who lived with me at that time, helped me to give my world a daily shape[78] and taught me how nice it is to go for walks. Walking can help you feel at home in the world. The world itself helps: the bigger and wider the surround-ings, whether in the form of an expansive vista or a forest, the stronger the feeling that I'm a part of everything, that things aren't so bad. A landscape can console you precisely because it lets you see and sense your own insignificance.

And one day I started running. For me, running is more important than walking—if I have an injury, then I have to go cycling. Running puts my thoughts and feelings in perspective, and even in good times makes everything just that bit lighter.[79] For the first ten or twenty minutes ticking thoughts about work and people and whatever else is bothering me keep going through my mind and shadowing my footsteps. After that it's as if the thoughts roll away like wheels, come to a stop, and merge into my surroundings. I can see a houseboat, and two coots—the second is calling to the first one—there's a man sitting on a bench drinking beer (I often run along the River

Amstel)—trees have twisty arms, light breaks on the water. My footsteps follow each other and the rhythm carries me, not the other way round: I am running, I no longer have to do much about it. Running slowly pounds the tension from my body, possible knots from my stomach. When it's over the day is more bearable, my body lighter. Running every other day is usually enough, but if anxiety or grief have settled somewhere in my body, I can always choose to do more.[80]

The French philosopher Maurice Merleau-Ponty claims that thinking is embodied.[81] How and what we think is always, of necessity, influenced by our physical being in the world.[82] We can't perceive ourselves or our environment from some point up in the air; we exist as bodies. If I decide to go running, it may look as if my head is controlling my body, but these are interlocking cogs. If I feel more at home in the world after running, that's because I can feel my feet, and feel the ground with my feet, and so I can better understand why I'm here. I also write best when I don't think too much, if I let my fingers find the words of their own accord, if I don't ask myself if my thoughts are correct. I do have to think about it later, but to let something new come into existence, I must follow my body. In *The Shaking Woman or A History of My Nerves* Siri Hustvedt describes something similar: that many writers see themselves as being a conduit between the story, or the book, and the rest of the world. That is almost magical thinking, but for me, at any rate, it seems impossible to write something myself—I can only follow the story that presents itself and I never have a complete grip on it.

Merleau-Ponty also points to the importance of habits. Acquiring new habits expands the way we are rooted in the world. For me, going for walks has become a habit, just like running; these are things that are simply part of life and that help me. (You can see a parallel with behavioural therapy here, which is also about teaching yourself new habits.) Habits belong to the body and to time; they belong to the background of our lives. We share habits with the other animals. Going for walks is a habit, just like having breakfast. Moreover, cultivating good habits can be a form of resistance to what happens to us, comparable to what Foucault calls practices of the self; not therapy, but ethos—improving yourself out of necessity.[83]

The memory-body and recurrent depression

In the month I turned thirty my grandmother died; the person I was in love with didn't want to be with me any more; and I walked in on a good friend in the aftermath of a suicide attempt. Up to then, I'd always slept reasonably well, except during the anorexic period; I need quite a lot of sleep and sleep has always helped me to process things. This sequence of events, however, meant that I could no longer get a single night of uninterrupted sleep. Things went from bad to worse: I ended up hardly sleeping at all; if I was lucky, I got a few hours per night, often between twelve and three. I learnt that in spring the blackbirds start singing before four o'clock in the morning, and that a continuous lack of sleep is guaranteed to cause gloom. It's as if my body has now taught itself this habit: since then I often sleep badly when I'm worried and the worries that come haunting me at night are always bigger than those of the day.

At first it went reasonably well. Mourning gives a framework, a shape for feelings, and I knew what my sadness was about. The death of my grandma, whom I really loved, was tightly bound in my mind to my aunt's death, long before; for all of us the grief pointed back to that grief, making it harder to bear. My friend was admitted to a clinic and taken care of, and she took charge of making herself better. The break-up turned out to be only a short one, and the relationship continued to simmer on for a few more years, sometimes as friendship, sometimes as love, until (fortunately) it was really broken.

But the shock proved to have settled into my body. My skin held blood, flesh, bones and muscles together, and concealed a gaping hole. Not sleeping caused tension and misery during the day; tension and misery that in their turn made it harder to sleep. By the time I could sleep again, six months later, at some point that summer, I'd been completely taken over by the familiar grittiness I associate with the start of a depression. It feels like static on a TV screen, grey but still moving. I began to function like a machine, determined to keep busy, wearing a mask during social interactions, swimming in fatigue—it's a real effort to keep doing things when the Earth has a stronger pull on you than usual.

Unlike my earlier episodes of depression, I wasn't really suicidal. By 'wasn't really' I mean that I had no plans for it. Death, in my experience, is always close at hand when you're depressed—perhaps depression is a kind of down payment on death, because life has been put on hold—but that doesn't mean the person who is depressed actually wants to die. Because depression paralyses, suicide is often far away, and anyway when you're depressed you can think two things at once. I knew I wasn't worth bothering about and I knew that this thought was part of my condition. So I just kept on moving.

According to Merleau-Ponty the living body is composed of two layers: the present body and the habit body.

The habit body lifts what we have achieved in the past—our skills, habits, our particular way of seeing the world, our attitudes, and so forth—into the present, so we can encounter it. We live in time, in every moment given to us, and in the fact that time is always in motion. What we have lived through has become a part of us and colours our experience, lifts us up, helps us to see—and relationships with others also broaden how we perceive and what we see. This doesn't mean that memories are static. They grow with us. Events, or memories, may not vanish, but they do discolour, twist and transform.

During my last depression, which followed the time I described above, my body seemed to be filled with concrete rubble. Every morning I cycled to the park on an old, heavy cargo trike with Pika the dog in the box—it was too far for her to walk– and that journey seemed to take hours, as did the stroll that followed. Sometimes it felt as if I was walking with my chin just above the ground, because everything was dragging me down. But I did walk, day after day, and Pika walked beside me. At home I drank coffee, studied and worked, and kept myself and my life moving. After a few months, the fog still hadn't lifted; and heaviness always has a tendency to get heavier because fighting fatigues you. I went to my doctor, who said that the medicine cupboard was always open for me, but she thought I could manage without. On her advice I visited a lute-playing psychotherapist—he told me he played the lute, he didn't play it for me. He turned out not to be covered by my medical insurance, so I only went once, but he still sent me a big bill, because the consultation had apparently included drawing up a treatment plan. I was very poor in those days, so that was all I could afford.

What helped me to move on, apart from running (slow running, step by step) and walking with Pika, was the thought that I could still commit suicide, that it was a real option, and that the doctor's medicine cabinet was open for me. The latter option would be my first step if things got worse. The fact that external circumstances played a part in this—a love relationship going up in smoke, money worries—helped me put my thoughts in perspective. There were reasons; people do react to these kinds of things. I could switch between what I was thinking and feeling and an abstract image of the future. I didn't think that things would improve in the future, but working from a logic that came from my previous experience—it had been bad before and it had got better—I could hold open the possibility that things would improve, or else there were alternatives. So this wasn't a hope that things would get better, but rather an awareness that the possibility of hope existed. There were some very dark days and I wasn't really present, but luckily the real depths didn't last all that long. A few months, and then things slowly grew lighter.

My body is made up of everything I have experienced, and everything I now experience resonates against that background. Old feelings are like the bottom of the sea more than the strata of the Earth: they're stirred up by new feelings and then settle again, but just that little bit differently. The new feeling is never completely new—maybe it was once like that, when you first fell in love, at the first break-up, and all those other first times—but now it's mingled with how it was. That is the duality of growing older: events that were previously earth-shattering are now known, fall into grooves scored by previous events, and so they're easier to put into perspective, although it can be precisely this that makes them much worse. The first time you lose someone lovable means the end of a world—the world that suddenly came into being when you met that person; if this happens more often, it becomes a part of your world—which apparently is a place where others come and go, where loss happens. Something like this also happens with being depressed. The first time really is an end, a stumbling block, a wall so high that you can't see over it. Later, being depressed becomes part of the fixed view. That doesn't make it any less paralysing, but it does make it different. Growing older and having often been depressed brings resignation with it, in my experience, which can be helpful (it will pass; it can pass, as it did before; today's a bad day, but that will also pass). The focus shifts from wanting to get better to simply enduring. At the same time, this way of seeing it can make me even sadder, because apparently this will never stop.

Animal helpers

As well as my work, and running and walking, the animals who live with me have helped me get through the depressions of the past ten years. At the moment I live with two dogs; before that I lived with a cat and a different dog. Without them I wouldn't have pulled through (and that applies to many other people as well; the positive effect of companion animals on depression and on other psychological impediments has been scientifically proven).[84] They were with me when I couldn't tolerate other people, without asking or wanting anything I couldn't give.[85] They were and are always happy to see me, and being appreciated like that can make all the difference. There's a common belief that companion animals depend on human beings, and that is sometimes given as one of the reasons for discounting their point of view, and why they're seen as being inferior to humans. This is debatable, in fact—cats are quite able to survive without people, and many dogs could learn to do so too—but it also doesn't

EVA MEIJER

recognize that humans need other animals, human or nonhuman. This is much more than having someone to care for, to come home to, to do my utmost for. It's about having someone who notices how you feel, who comes and sits beside you if things get worse and doesn't go away, who loves you even if you don't say anything, even if you're always crying, and can't do anything good in the world. Of course, there are ways in which contact between humans is special, but so is contact with other animals. My soft, white cat Putih, who was Lebanese and had lived through a war, would sit on my lap as I wrote my first books, slept under the bedcovers with me, and purred when I stroked him because I couldn't sleep. That kind of closeness is incredibly comforting and important. It was also mutual: I sat with him when he was feeling sick, or needed medicine and I'd stroke his fur if that was what he wanted. This is also true of the dogs I now live with: I look after them; I work for their biscuits and take the younger one to courses; they look after me by keeping an eye on me, sitting beside me if something's going on, keeping me focused. We shape our shared life together, by going for walks, for example. Some choices I make alone, but they determine other things.

The western image of autonomy includes an atomistic view of people. That means that the individual has a central position, just as in the medical model I described in

106

the previous chapter, and it also means that the individual is perceived as something that precedes relationships and that can be independent of them. This is not so much an empirical observation as a normative interpretation of humans: independence and autonomy are better than dependency. That image is misleading. We are all born into relationships and depend on them in different ways throughout our lives, and when we enter into relationships with others, they too can become dependent on us. Parent-child relationships are a good example of dependency, of course, but there are many, more general ways in which we lean on one another. For example, we need our friends so we can talk about things, interpret them and sharpen our judgement, and to laugh with them or just keep each other company. Writers need editors to look critically at their books; academic philosophers need colleagues to assess their work; and so on and so forth. Someone who is depressed may need to lean even more on her environment, in the form of a doctor, psychiatrist, partner, pills, friends, or the dog. And that need can pass, and then others will lean on her. Dependency is graduated: it works differently for each individual and changes in the course of life. Everyone begins as a baby. And there is nothing wrong as such with a certain degree of dependence: relationships are a fount of richness, while loving someone means linking your destiny to that particular person, so that you partly become dependent on that person's well-being. Their happiness will in part become your own. Avoiding that would lead to a bare and chilly life.

As I've already said, it's difficult to connect to others during a depression. This is partly to do with the guilt you feel for being depressed. Because my mood was so low during my depressions, I often felt guilty about the animals, even though we were helping each other. Putih and Pika certainly saw and felt the dark clouds around me, and sometimes I was afraid that this affected their mood too. I never neglected them or deprived them in any way and perhaps the feeling of guilt was also prompted by my state of mind and alienation. But they were my link to life, they looked after me, and that's a heavy burden for furry friends.[86]

If you love someone, you want them to be happy, and as I've already mentioned, happiness isn't something that is often associated with me. We can't always help others. Sometimes we can, and sometimes in ways that we didn't foresee—before Pika, I hadn't expected that living with a dog would bring me so much, or that walking would play such a big role. But there are depths that others can't reach. Perhaps I'm not an easy person for other people to be with because I'm always lugging that weight. This isn't really expressed in anger or petulance, but in a shadow that sometimes envelops me, which isn't always possible to write or laugh away. There were times when I cancelled quite a few appointments, because I really couldn't face them. That has improved now: I understand better what I can and can't do and I stick to that—I've grown more accustomed to myself. But there are still moments when I'm absent, when I withdraw. I once thought I should carry on seeing people—I now know that this isn't necessary as long as I keep moving, and that it's just a part of me to sometimes be like that. Sometimes it's better to go into hiding than stand in the full light of day.

Winter trees

Depression makes everything still—yourself and the world. Although pain can seem like screaming, it is emptiness that intrudes. It may seem that you should fight this with music or brightly coloured paintings, but stillness works better, in my experience.

My need for stillness—a minimum of people, images and noises—is greater than average. I need time when very little happens around me, to work, and to process what has happened. As a machine processes raw materials into an end product, I mean, and not like someone processing a trauma. Empty days, when I go for walks and write and maybe bake a loaf of bread, are necessary to compensate for the full days, with meetings, talks and teaching. A world without people but with trees, cats, birds, grants space. Rest does me good when I've worked hard, as long as I can rest at home, on the sofa.[87]

I love black-and-white—bare, black winter trees against a white sky, print on paper, pencil drawings, sad singer-songwriter songs, Wittgenstein's remarks, Armando's landscapes, Bach's Inventions, coffee in my white mug, crows in the snow. Perhaps because I feel so much of everything around me, and often overflow with it, perhaps because I see something of my own life in them. My movement towards silence is not a retreat from the world, it's about making time, stretching it, making it my own, precisely to keep meeting that world with openness. Walking is a good way of doing that, writing too, and meditating (constantly returning to where you are, giving the background noise a stern talking-to and then setting it aside, learning to feel at home in the moments that constitute the now). The resistance is also aimed at our society, which is so loud, and at something deeper, the slipping away of the days. If you don't watch out, everything will have passed. Being attentive is perhaps the only weapon against that.

Depression makes the world whiter. Not like snow—snow shows us so beautifully that the world is bigger than us. Depression doesn't cover up, it erases. The louder and more cheerful the outside world, the stronger the contrast. Wearing silence around you like a cloak isn't something that can quite prepare you for that, but practising with it can help you learn to deal with emptiness. And when you're quiet you can look better, see better how everything changes, and in this way you stay closer to time.

5

On steadfastness and rooting yourself in the world: by way of a conclusion

According to the Stoics, everything that will happen in the world is already fixed; people can't do anything about that. We are, however, free to determine our own response to events. This response is crucial for our own happiness. This doesn't mean that you can just sit back and let life wash over you. On the contrary, you should train yourself in various situations to see whether you can change things or not, and, if you can't, accept what is happening. Everyone should strive for happiness and that is the best way of doing so, the Stoics think. We like to believe that everything can be mended, but that isn't the case. Things break, and there's nothing we can do about it.

We can learn from the Stoics that you just have to bear some of the things that happen to you. Perhaps you can't always bear a depression: it seems strange to talk about bearing it when something extremely heavy has leapt on top of you and pushed you down to the ground, so you can't stand up again—but enduring it does have value. Being able to get through a day, or an hour, or even a few minutes, in bed or out of it, could be your greatest ever achievement. That day will pass, and the next day too, regardless of whether you move and whether or not a light is switched on. It happens to you, and you can respond by accepting that. Just lean on time, because there is little else you can do.

At the end of her poem 'Having it Out with Melancholy', the American poet Jane Kenyon describes a morning in June.[88] She wakes up at four, the wood thrush starts singing, and she is suddenly overwhelmed with a feeling of 'ordinary contentment'. (I know exactly what she means by 'ordinary contentment': the contentment that normal people feel, who have a life without depression, and who don't have to spend all their time trying so hard to do their best.) All at once, the bird's swift little heart and gleaming eye put everything to rights again—why did things hurt so much before? As swiftly as the storm blows up, it can also vanish. What is terrible about repeated depressions is, of course, that the threat remains and that remnants are left behind, like floating patches of ice after a spell of frost, but sometimes it's suddenly fine again, for a while. And

113

you can try to accept the rest. By acceptance I don't mean just giving up. It's about being steadfast, and connecting your destiny to the world as much as you can.

Being steadfast

'Resolution and constancy do not lay down as a law that we may not protect ourselves, as far as it lies in our power to do so, from the ills and misfortunes which threaten us, nor consequently that we should not fear that they may surprise us,' Montaigne says in his essay 'On constancy'.[89] On the contrary, retreat can sometimes be the best battle tactic, and if disaster can't be averted, then it should be patiently endured. A large part of my life is organized around the quirks of my psyche: walking, running, going to bed early, not drinking much alcohol (luckily, I like going to bed early and being a frugal drinker, and walking and running too, for that matter—I do have a somewhat ascetic streak—but I do it all with an iron discipline). Perhaps avoiding falling in love, if I can, is part of this too—where some people just fall flat and then carry on, emotional intensities can really throw me off balance. It's beside the point whether it's a successful union, or one where it's soon obvious that things will come unstuck because two intense personalities just double the problems—it unbalances me, and I can only permit that for something really important. Love always presents itself as being really important, of course, and that's something you also have to obey; love is a mainstay of life and gives it meaning. And maybe you can't choose love, because love chooses you, though you can often choose not to yield to it. In any case, you simply can't avoid being caught in a storm, so stand firm, be steadfast.

The same is true for the storm of depression. There are mornings that are impossible to get through. Sometimes these are followed by afternoons that twist inwards and always last longer than normal, that have thorns (you can feel them on the inside of your skin). These in their turn can be followed by evenings when things only get worse (things can always be worse). These are just bad days. It's enough to get through them, you don't have to do anything with them—you're still yourself, it's just the day that's against you. It doesn't matter if you can't work, if you don't want to talk to people, if your house is the only safe place left. Just tell yourself: this is a bad day, a day that shouldn't have happened. Soon you'll go to sleep, then you'll be taken to another place, and when you come back, everything will start anew. Anew: a word that carries both repetition and renewal, which you should try to make your friend.

Lifebuoys: fictive or factual

The annoying thing about depression is that there isn't always anything you can do about it. The insights that therapy gives can help you move on, especially if there are concrete reasons for being depressed, and self-knowledge may be useful for many aspects of life. But depression isn't always something you can solve with your head. With recurrent depressions in particular, it's more important to develop habits and techniques to help you to endure them, to make sure you have a safety net of humans and animals who look after you and who you can look after, and to keep busy. Constantly having to fight for breathing space is exhausting, but there's not much else you can do.

You can try to train yourself to withstand episodes of depression and to put your own unhappiness in perspective. I don't mean that these shouldn't be taken seriously, but that you should try as much as possible to live with them. With mild depression it can be very important to keep working, for as long as you can. You can't see the point of your life, but others do see your value, and at least work offers some distraction and then you've got through another day. Latch on to what you want or wanted to do and to the arrangements you've made with others. Acting 'as if' can help you get through your days, to get where you want to be—in the same way that being brave isn't any kind of immense, passionate feeling that will inevitably carry you through difficulties, but is more about managing to go through and beyond the fear. Do it, if something seems worthwhile to you. The future isn't fixed.

Art is a thread running through my life and through this book. It's one of the weapons we have against point-lessness, a way of giving meaning to what is actually there and what could possibly be. When someone sees the world differently, it changes; and the artist is the magician who can show things in a different way. For me, it's necessary to make things and I'm lucky I can do so. But depression is the great equalizer: if things are really not going well, then all of this seems, or really is, worth nothing. Then the hope is that my roots, with which I grow into the earth, are strong enough to keep me standing.

The world is big

Steadfastness has to do with being rooted in the world. 'World' is an important concept in phenomenology. It sig-nifies not so much the planet on which we live, but rather the communal life-worlds into which we are born and which we shape with others. Humans, and other animals too, are always actively shaping their environments, so that when you meet others and your lives become wrapped around each other, a shared world comes into being.

When you can't heal yourself, helping others can be helpful. It's good for them and it's a way in which you can give meaning to your own life. Instead of valuing life in terms of happiness, fulfilled goals, or contentment, you could evaluate it in terms of the work you do for others. Not because of prestige or ego, but because of the other, who does still have worth. You then have a general usefulness, instead of being only of no use to yourself, and you're building something, you're making something whole. This is how we can help each other, also because, as I've already mentioned, our societies really need love and care. People who do voluntary work in animal shelters are a good example of how this could work. At the Amsterdam Foundation for Stray Cats, where I worked for some time as a volunteer, many of the volunteers there carry their own baggage. For some of them, cleaning out the pens or socializing the cats is the only time they go out that day or that week, and it's what keeps them going. The cats benefit from this, and they play an active role in the healing process: cleaning bike sheds or repairing televisions could never have the same effect. Encounters with others contain hope—even if, or perhaps especially if, those others are furry and are crazy about fish. Activism can help too. Attach your heart to a cause, make sure that it becomes a part of your own destiny. Because you won't pull through, if the only thing you are is depressed. Committing yourself to something important is a form of resistance, not only against unjust social structures, but also against your own sinking away. We are linked to each other, the world is our home. And writing can help to enlarge this worldhood. You don't necessarily have to go outside for this, although often the most important advice I give to others is to literally keep moving.

As I've already discussed, there is no clear dividing line between being mad and being normal. That distinction changes over time and differs between cultures, and there are also valuable sides to depression. People who get depressed have a special understanding of the meaninglessness and absurdity of existence, an insight that puts the herd behaviour of many people into perspective, for example, or the fetishization of money. Depression shows you something about the world that some people never get to see. We are alone here, that's just how it is, even if we share that aloneness with everyone else. The experiences that let you see that life can't be taken for granted also give it depth.

This isn't much use to you when you're in an acute depressive episode, but there are things you can hold onto: time, which persists in moving forward, and which moves you too; the dog who lays her head on your thigh;

119

the thought that everything can once more change. The beauty of this is that these things hold you up as well, even when you can't sense it.

The world is big. Far bigger than you and far older. The sun keeps rising, each time anew, and it keeps on setting too. The trees in the nearby woods have stood there for more than a hundred years now; you can touch their trunks. The seashore shows you that it doesn't matter if you're there or not. Whether you're found or whether you're lost, the waves keep moving; the surf recedes and then returns; the sea doesn't end, it simply merges into the sky in the distance. Your body is also a sea, moving along with the day and the night, it gets older of its own accord, is made of particles that are much older than you. Soon everything will be over and you will be absorbed into what was. So lean on the earth then, on the days that carry you. Tomorrow could be different.

NOTES

1   I found a website on the internet with information about historical weather, which showed that 1994 was mostly a rainy year. It's true that the summer was hot, but May wasn't particularly sunny. I probably noticed the sun because of the other events I describe here.

2   Jean-Paul Sartre, *Nausea*. Penguin Books, 1976 [1938].

3   Albert Camus, *The Myth of Sisyphus and Other Essays*. Vintage Books, 1991 [1942].

4   William Styron, who I'll return to later, says in *Darkness Visible: A Memoir of Madness* (Vintage, 2004, p. 21) that Camus also struggled with depression. He wonders whether Camus' death in a car accident was actually a form of suicide, because he consciously chose to travel with someone known to be a reckless driver.

5   Going wrong can also turn out well. Kevin Hines jumped off the Golden Gate Bridge as a teenager,

intending to take his own life, and was saved by a sea lion. His story can be found on the internet: 'San Francisco bridge jumper says sea lion saved him', AFP, *The Telegraph.*

6   Art provides a glimmer of hope in Sartre's *Nausea*, as it also does for Camus, but perhaps this is simply a popular illusion.

7   It works the other way round too: my sensitivity, perhaps the main reason why I get depressed, is also the reason why I can make the work I make. My vulnerability actually is my strongest weapon, even though that may seem a cliché. My borders are porous; my skin is no wall. What is outside can easily flow in, and what is inside me will always find its way out. To create work, this constant back-and-forth between the world and the self is necessary.

8   Eva Meijer, *Dagpauwoog*. Cossee, 2013. This novel has not yet been translated into English.

9   In her memoir, *Paradoxical Undressing* (Atlantic Books, 2011), Hersh describes how the songs come from outside of her and surround her with their clamour, and how she then has to play them to get rid of the noise. You can hear it in her music—Hersh creates a strange world that is both a desert and a sea, a place where you can catch your breath, but where you're also constantly under threat. Making music demands

absolute presence, and Hersh also demands that of the listener.

10   For me, singing has never been a way of expressing happiness—people sometimes think you must be really happy if you sing on your bike. But for me it's much more about continuing to exist, hearing that I still have a voice.

11   Fernando Pessoa writes a lot about this feeling of simultaneously existing and not existing. 'For months I have not been alive,' he says in Fragment 139 of his *Book of Disquiet* (Penguin Books, 2015). He hardly dreams, has written nothing for a long time, and although he fulfils his duties at the office, his thinking and feeling have come to a standstill. 'Alas, that does not mean peace: decay is also a process.' Suicide seems a questionable way of solving his deep sense of weariness with life; death isn't enough because it's about the feeling that he never wanted to exist. He tries to cure this longing by writing, which according to him is an 'ironic cure', only suitable for the few.

12   Mendieta died young, having fallen from the window of her 34th-floor apartment. According to the neighbours she'd had a violent argument with her partner, the celebrated artist Carl Andre, just before her death. He was tried for her murder, but acquitted for lack of evidence.

13   Jacques Derrida has said that we can't erase our traces
      and can't control them. What we leave behind will
      irrevocably take on a life of its own. This is true on a
      large scale, as in the case of a novel that every reader
      will read differently, coming to it with a different
      background, but also on a smaller scale, such as with
      the comments that strangers carry with them, or the
      things we give or say to our loved ones, which change
      their meaning over time. Meaning is always fluid.
      What has happened acquires a new tone because
      of what happens afterwards; in films and books this
      can lead to a conclusion, a feeling of completion at
      the end. People like conclusions and fully rounded
      stories, and so they're inclined to interpret their own
      lives in this way too. In the beautiful little book *The
      Red Notebook and other writings* (Faber and Faber, 1995),
      Paul Auster writes about chance happenings in his
      life and shows that there is actually no real difference
      between chance and destiny. What happens had to
      happen and that is something we simply have to deal
      with. The patterns we discover are our own patterns,
      but that doesn't make them less true.

14   Art acquires significance from and for everyone who
      comes in contact with it. My work, therefore, is much
      bigger than I am, and is uncontrollable: every viewer,
      reader, or listener makes something different of it. It

is also uncontrollable because it compels itself; I have never had any control over what I make. It is precisely because it is unfamiliar, something that comes from outside of me, and is more important than I am, that it can sometimes carry me.

15 For me, writing this essay is also cyclical: it takes me back to the artists, writers and musicians who were once important to me. The feeling these evoke is like meeting an old friend: both of you are older and wiser (sadder but wiser), and you reminisce together, and talk about the new things that have happened. You're pleased to see each other again, but it's sad too, because you've grown a little apart and in the other's ageing you can see the evanescence of everything.

16 I've always felt a link in this respect to the early feminist performance artists of the sixties and seventies.

17 Tracey Emin, *Strangeland*. Sceptre, 2005.

18 Jeanette Winterson's review of *Strangeland* can be read on her website: www.jeanettewinterson.com

19 Skye Sherwin, 'Tracey Emin's My Bed: A violent mess of sex and death', *The Guardian*.

20 I discuss this in more detail in Chapter 3. See Simon Kyaga, *Creativity and Mental Illness: The Mad Genius in Question*. Springer, 2014.

21 Patricia De Martelaere, 'De levenskunstenaar, naar een esthetiek van zelfmoord' [The life-artist, towards

an aesthetics of suicide] in *Een verlangen naar ontroost-baarheid* [A Longing for Inconsolability]. Meulenhoff, 2003.

22 Ibid. p. 100.

23 William Styron, *Darkness Visible: A Memoir of Madness.* Open Road Media, 2010.

24 In *All Men are Mortal* (Virago, 1995 [1946]) Simone de Beauvoir shows that immortality isn't a solution either. The main character of the story is immortal, and this gives him a very accurate picture of human beings, because he has long been familiar with them. In the course of time, however, he is no longer a real human, being unable to love others. He only sees their impermanence.

25 I don't think depression is a specifically philosoph-ical illness—it can affect anyone—but in my expe-rience the emptiness it gives rise to, the emptiness that spreads out from it, is linked to these kinds of thoughts. Moreover, the self-doubt accompanying depression has something philosophical about it. In any case, to doubt supposed certainties has been an accepted method of investigation since the time of Descartes. To apply this method to your own life or worth may be somewhat exaggerated, but it is valid.

26 Kari Van Hoorick, 'Wat depressie met onze hersenen doet' [What depression does to our brain]. *Knack*, 2017.

27 Sophia Bennett and Alan J. Thomas, 'Depression and Dementia: Cause, Consequence or Coincidence?' *Maturitas* 79.2 (2014): 184–190.

28 Josine Verhoeven investigates this phenomenon in her doctoral thesis *Depression, Anxiety and Cellular Aging: Does Feeling Blue Make You Grey?* (Vrije Universiteit Amsterdam, 2016).

29 Ray Monk, *Ludwig Wittgenstein: The Duty of Genius*. Penguin Books, 1991.

30 Ludwig Wittgenstein, *Tractatus logico-philosophicus*. Routledge, 2001 [1922].

31 I am mainly thinking here about the *Philosophical Investigations* (Basil Blackwell Ltd, 1958), but the same applies to the other later texts, particularly the various 'remarks'.

32 Imagine a street at four o'clock on a Tuesday morning, with a pale yellow light from the streetlamps. The dog is ill and we're on our way to the river so she can relieve herself in the grass by the waterside. There's no one outside and it is as if no one was ever there; even the ghosts prefer to stay inside. This may seem unusual for a while, but it doesn't have to stay like that.

33 *The White Book* by Han Kang (Granta Books, 2017) is an exploration of the colour white, which is actually about loss—not the various disconnected experiences of loss which we can all identify or talk about to each

other, but the loss that is part of the basic structure of our existence.

34 The longing to get better, to see the point of life and enjoy it, is valuable in and of itself because it holds a promise, it gives you something to strive for—not hope as such perhaps, but the possibility of hope—just as we need the promise of understanding to wish to use language at all, as Wittgenstein points out.

35 Sunaura Taylor, *Beasts of Burden: Animal and Disability Liberation*. The New Press, 2017.

36 Michel Foucault, *The Care of the Self: The History of Sexuality, Vol. 3*. Pantheon, 1986.

37 Kevin A. Aho, 'Depression and Embodiment: Phenomenological Reflections on Motility, Affectivity, and Transcendence'. *Medicine, Health Care and Philosophy* 16.4 (2013): 751–759.

38 Martin Heidegger, *Being and Time*. Blackwell Publishing Ltd, 1962. See also: Martin Heidegger, *The Fundamental Concepts of Metaphysics: World, Finitude, Solitude*. Indiana University Press, 1995.

39 Jacques Derrida, *The Beast and the Sovereign, Volume I and II (The Seminars of Jacques Derrida)*. The University of Chicago Press, 2009/2011.

40 As well as a film based on an earlier (lost) film, the artwork includes photos and postcards. My discussion here is about the Dutch film of 1971.

41 For example, the Dutch journalist Betty van Garrel wrote in the *Haagse Post* (1972) that Ader was sentimental, 'a romantic softie', and 'not even original'.

42 Because reading takes time—its duration is an element of the work—the novel, in comparison to other art forms, is pre-eminently suited to the evocation of moods.

43 Seneca, *De goede dood* [The good death]. Uitgeverij Athenaeum-Polak & Van Gennep, 2015. See also: Seneca, *Letters on Ethics*. The University of Chicago Press, 2015/2017; Seneca, *Dialogues and Letters*. Penguin Books, 1997.

44 The rotatory swing and its effects is described in detail in Mason Cox's *Practical Observations on Insanity*. 2nd edition. C. and R. Baldwin; J. Murray, 1806, pp. 137–176.

45 See Chapters V and VI of Michel Foucault's *Madness and Civilization: A History of Insanity in the Age of Reason*. Vintage Books, 1988. This book is discussed in more detail later in this chapter.

46 Hysteria, for example, a typical female disease, was ascribed to the idea that the uterus trotted around the body (Foucault, 1988; Chapter V). Mad women have often been forcibly sterilized, both in the past and current times. See, for example: Kathryn Krase, 'History of Forced Sterilization and Current U.S. Abuses'.

47   Wouter Kusters, *A Philosophy of Madness: The Experience of Psychotic Thinking*. MIT, 2020 (forthcoming).

48   Quite a bit has been written about Kafka's eating habits, including by Kafka himself. Some people believe he was anorexic; see, for example: M.M. Fichter (1987). 'The anorexia nervosa of Franz Kafka'. *International Journal of Eating Disorders*, 6(3), 367–377.

49   I would like to give a special mention here to the smoking room. Wouter Kusters, in *A Philosophy of Madness*, points to the similarities between the philosophical symposium and the institutional smoking room, and he has a point. The great questions of life are discussed in both places, as if life itself depended on this.

50   The statistics in this paragraph are from the Dutch website proud2bme, which also includes plenty of information and help for people with eating disorders and their families and friends. In the UK similar information is available on the Beat Eating Disorders and the Anorexia & Bulimia Care websites.

51   I first read Descartes when I was thirteen, on the top floor of the library in my home town of Hoorn, and I recognized his aloneness in the *Meditations* as my own.

52   I recovered well from my eating disorder, in fact, and have never had a relapse since I was admitted to the clinic in 2000. It's a myth that anorexia can't

be cured, one that is cherished by anorexia patients, possibly because of the attachment to the illness that I previously discussed.

53 Judging your own thoughts and learning to control them, in both cognitive behavioural therapy and philosophy, is similar to meditation, in which stray thoughts are put inside brackets, with the aim of paying attention to what is important, or to what is simply there.

54 I use the term 'psychotherapy' here as shorthand for various forms of psychoanalytic and client-oriented psychotherapy, a cluster of approaches which are based on intensive individual conversations.

55 Freud wonders, with good reason, why letting go is so painful. Why does it cause people so much grief? It would be far more efficient if that wasn't the case.

56 Patricia De Martelaere, *Een verlangen naar ontroostbaarheid* [A Longing for Inconsolability]. Meulenhoff, 2003.

57 The studies showing that antidepressants can actually make young people suicidal were only published fifteen years or so later.

58 Andrea Cipriani, et al. 'Comparative Efficacy and Acceptability of 21 Antidepressant Drugs for the Acute Treatment of Adults with Major Depressive Disorder: A Systematic Review and Network Meta-Analysis'. *The Lancet* 391.10128 (2018): 1357–1366.

59   Information derived from medical insurance companies and from pharmacies confirms this. See: Margot Smolenaars, 'Anyone reading this is (not) crazy. Psychological problems are not black and white' on the website of the Dutch Research Council (NWO).

60   See footnote 58.

61   Ann Cvetkovich, *Depression: A Public Feeling.* Duke University Press, 2012.

62   Theodore L. Caputi, Davey Smith and John W. Ayers, 'Suicide Risk Behaviors Among Sexual Minority Adolescents in the United States, 2015'. *Jama* 318.23 (2017): 2349–2351.

63   Chelsey B. Coombs, 'Black People in New York Suffer from Depression More Than Any Other Group in the City'. *Gizmodo*, 2015.

64   Anni Ferguson, '"The lowest of the stack": why black women are struggling with mental health'. *The Guardian*, 2016.

65   Ewen Callaway, 'Fearful Memories Haunt Mouse Descendants'. *Nature*, 1 December 2013.

66   Alize J. Ferrari et al., 'Burden of Depressive Disorders by Country, Sex, Age, and Year: Findings from the Global Burden of Disease Study 2010.' *PLoS medicine* 10.11 (2013): e1001547.

67   The feminist animal philosopher Carol Adams clearly explains on her website what kinds of problems

'traumatic knowledge' can cause. See: Carol Adams, 'Traumatic Knowledge and Animal Exploitation: Part 1: What Is It?'

68 Greg Kelly, 'Modern-Day Plague: Understanding the Scope of Veterinary Suicide'.

69 The British writer Mark Fisher (1968–2017) argued something similar. His work demonstrates the links between political-economic structures and depression, and regards capitalism as an enormous problem for mental health. See, for example, Mark Fisher, *Capitalist Realism: Is There No Alternative?* Zero Books, 2009.

70 Unfortunately, depression is not limited to human beings: nonhuman animals can also get depressed. For example, depression has been discovered in salmon living in tightly packed fish farms, in elephants, in animals kept for a long time in animal shelters, and in animals who are intensively farmed. Many zoos give antidepressants to the inhabitants. See, for example: Laurel Braitman, *Animal Madness: How Anxious Dogs, Compulsive Parrots, and Elephants in Recovery Help Us Understand Ourselves*. Simon and Schuster, 2014. A convincing article about animal suicide has recently been published: David M. Pena-Guzmán, 'Can nonhuman animals commit suicide?' *Animal Sentience: An Interdisciplinary Journal on Animal Feeling*. 2.20 (2017): 1.

71 The same holds true for emotion, nature and animality.

72 It isn't clear whether these ships of fools actually existed.

73 Madness and animality have often been linked, historically and conceptually. There is a persistent prejudice that both the mad and nonhuman animals are incapable of reason. Historically, mad people were often portrayed and treated as if they were animals; they were locked up and put in chains, for example.

74 For these reasons, the new academic discipline of mad studies focuses precisely on what we consider to be sane. Mad studies makes the experience of people who self-identify as being mad the centre of its focus, and tries to look beyond the normativity of the normal. Instead of perceiving everything deviant as being inferior and worthy of rejection, richness can be discovered in other experiences. Moreover, any kind of thinking based on a standard norm that measures everything else against it produces oppression. This form of critical thinking has its origins in disability studies and is related to critical race studies, women's studies, and animal studies. By investigating how our ideas about madness and normality have actually come about, we can critically assess them and, if necessary, adjust them. Mad studies can be found within various fields of the humanities, such as in law,

philosophy, and gender studies. This field of scholar-ship focuses on the experience, history, culture, politics and narratives of those who self-identify as being mad, such as psychiatric patients, the neurodiverse, people with learning disabilities, psychotic people, or those with a history of psychiatric illness. This approach is also political: it questions contemporary thinking about madness and the societal practices connected to this, such as exclusion at social, economic, political or other levels.

75 In saying this I don't wish to deny that there are people who are seriously mentally ill and who need temporary or permanent professional help.

76 Derrida argues that this also applies to refugees, who are often perceived as a problem, or as something negative, whereas those who come from an outside into an inside (regardless of their intrinsic value and rights) hold a mirror up to us. We can see ourselves in what is strange; we can see ourselves as being strange. See: Jacques Derrida, *Of Hospitality: Anne Dufourmantelle Invites Jacques Derrida to Respond*. Stanford University Press, 2012.

77 See note 20.

78 Memories of earlier lives always reflect fragments, never the whole: there are always memories that seem to characterize a particular period, but you

will know which those are in retrospect. I used to go with Pika every week to the beach. We lived in one of the suburbs of The Hague, right by a dreary shopping centre, and from there we would take a bus to Kijkduin. We'd walk to the beach through the dunes, then some way along the sand, then back again. The sea always comforted me, and it's so moving to see a dog running towards you as fast as she possibly can. On the way back, Pika used to like pressing her wet body against the legs of some elderly fellow passenger (she would swim in the winter too). Once home, I'd give her salty head a kiss and then she'd sleep for the rest of the day while I was working. I was regularly unhappy at that time, especially in matters of love, and I worried a lot about money too, but this was the greatest feeling you could ever have of belonging: the dog, the sea, being together.

79 Research has shown that running can have a positive effect on mild and moderate depression (and anxiety disorders). In the case of severe depressions, its effectiveness has not been proven. Some people swear by it, like the well-known Dutch psychiatrist Bram Bakker, who is also a runner, and various institutions offer 'running therapy'. This article, by a moderately depressive runner, covers a lot of the current research: Scott Douglas, 'For Depression and Anxiety, Running

Is a Unique Therapy'. *Runner's World*. Nevertheless, running isn't a miracle cure and doesn't work for everyone.

80 Before taking up running I used to play the piano a lot; many roads lead to Rome.

81 Maurice Merleau-Ponty, *Phenomenology of Perception*. Routledge, 2012.

82 Humans aren't the only animals rooted in the world like this. I got to know Olli, a Romanian street dog who started living with me in 2013, partly through his physical reactions to events and to being touched. His body is covered in scars and he has lost half an ear. Shoes, stamping, cigarettes, and abrupt movements all scare him. It was completely new for him to live in a house: in his first week with me he clambered onto the kitchen worktop several times (he's a large dog, weighing twenty-three kilos) and jumped across the fence into the neighbour's garden. He gets food cans open by himself, and inspects human beings, both inside and outside the house: have they got food? Do they want to stroke him? When he's in the tram he says hello to everyone: he wants to find out if they're friends or enemies. He had to learn how to read me as well; my gestures weren't easy for him to understand, and they still aren't, unlike for a dog who has grown up with humans. In the streets he watches the city birds,

the pigeons and jackdaws and crows, so he can locate food. He is afraid of wearing collars, because he was hauled off the streets by dog catchers, who used a pole with a metal snare that clasped round his neck. I know some of the stories about his past; he tells me the rest through his posture and behaviour. That behaviour changes. In the first few months he was constantly on guard, sleeping with one eye open. He's now able to relax completely and sleep very deeply, even lying on his back sometimes. He made no eye contact at all in the first six weeks, but now he looks at me when there's something exciting going on outside. But the fears are still shut inside him, and if it's thundering, or someone lets off a firework, or makes a sudden move towards him, he takes to his heels. The physiotherapist who treated him for knee problems was able to read his physical history in his body.

83 See note 36.

84 See this article for an overview: Marc Bekoff, 'Companion Animals Help People with Mental Health Problems', *Psychology Today*.

85 I want to make it clear here that I've been lucky in always having people who loved me and I've always had good friends.

86 Very little research has been carried out on the well-being of assistance dogs and other assistance

animals, but we do know that they have more problems with stress than other dogs. Because humans are increasingly making use of assistance animals, it is important to carry out more research on this. Lisa Maria Glenk, 'Current Perspectives on Therapy Dog Welfare in Animal-Assisted Interventions'. *Animals* 7.2 (2017): 7.

87   Silence is also a necessary reference point for creation. You need a good background if you want to add something to what is already there: a song must be better than silence; a drawing has to add something to all the images already in existence; this book should add to the experience of depression.

88   The poem was published in Kenyon's collection *Constance* (1993) and is available online.

89   Michel de Montaigne, *The Complete Essays*. Penguin Books, 2003. The essay 'On constancy' ('De la Constance') is translated into Dutch as 'Over standvastigheid' ('On steadfastness').

If you are affected by some of the issues discussed in this book, help is available. The Samaritans is a voluntary UK-based organization who will listen to your concerns. Calls are free on 116 123. More information about the service can be found on the Samaritans website: www. samaritans.org.

If you are concerned about eating disorders, support can be found on the Beat Eating Disorders website: www.beateatingdisorders.org.uk. The charity Anorexia & Bulimia Care is also a good source of support: www. anorexiabulimiacare.org.uk.